Number 146
Summer 2015

New Directions for Evaluation

Paul R. Brandon
Editor-in-Chief

Evaluation and Social Justice in Complex Sociopolitical Contexts

Barbara Rosenstein
Helena Desivilya Syna
Editors

Evaluation and Social Justice in Complex Sociopolitical Contexts
Barbara Rosenstein, Helena Desivilya Syna (eds.)
New Directions for Evaluation, no. 146
Paul R. Brandon, Editor-in-Chief

Copyright © 2015 Wiley Periodicals, Inc., A Wiley Company, and the American Evaluation Association. All rights reserved. No part of this publication may be reproduced in any form or by any means, except as permitted under sections 107 and 108 of the 1976 United States Copyright Act, without either the prior written permission of the publisher or authorization through the Copyright Clearance Center, 222 Rosewood Drive, Danvers, MA 01923; (978) 750-8400; fax (978) 646-8600. The copyright notice appearing at the bottom of the first page of a chapter in this journal indicates the copyright holder's consent that copies may be made for personal or internal use, or for personal or internal use of specific clients, on the condition that the copier pay for copying beyond that permitted by law. This consent does not extend to other kinds of copying, such as copying for general distribution, for advertising or promotional purposes, for creating collective works, or for resale. Such permission requests and other permission inquiries should be addressed to the Permissions Department, c/o John Wiley © Sons, Inc., 111 River Street, Hoboken, NJ 07030; (201) 748-6011, fax (201) 748-6008, www.wiley.com/go/permissions.

Microfilm copies of issues and articles are available in 16mm and 35mm, as well as microfiche in 105mm, through University Microfilms Inc., 300 North Zeeb Road, Ann Arbor, MI 48106-1346.

New Directions for Evaluation is indexed in Academic Search Alumni Edition (EBSCO Publishing), Education Research Complete (EBSCO Publishing), Higher Education Abstracts (Claremont Graduate University), SCOPUS (Elsevier), Social Services Abstracts (ProQuest), Sociological Abstracts (ProQuest), Worldwide Political Science Abstracts (ProQuest).

NEW DIRECTIONS FOR EVALUATION (ISSN 1097-6736, electronic ISSN 1534-875X) is part of The Jossey-Bass Education Series and is published quarterly by Wiley Subscription Services, Inc., A Wiley Company, at Jossey-Bass, One Montgomery Street, Suite 1200, San Francisco, CA 94104-4594.

SUBSCRIPTIONS for individuals cost $89 for U.S./Canada/Mexico/international. For institutions, $358 U.S.; $398 Canada/Mexico; $432 international. Electronic only: $89 for individuals all regions; $358 for institutions all regions. Print and electronic: $98 for individuals in the U.S., Canada, and Mexico; $122 for individuals for the rest of the world; $430 for institutions in the U.S.; $470 for institutions in Canada and Mexico; $504 for institutions for the rest of the world.

All issues are proposed by guest editors. For proposal submission guidelines, go to http://www.eval.org/p/cm/ld/fid=48. Editorial correspondence should be addressed to the Editor-in-Chief, Paul R. Brandon, University of Hawai'i at Mānoa, 1776 University Avenue, Castle Memorial Hall Rm 118, Honolulu, HI 96822-2463.

www.josseybass.com

Cover photograph by ©iStock.com/Smithore

New Directions for Evaluation

Sponsored by the American Evaluation Association

Editor-in-Chief
Paul R. Brandon   University of Hawai'i at Mānoa

Associate Editors
J. Bradley Cousins   University of Ottawa
Lois-ellin Datta   Datta Analysis

Editorial Advisory Board

Anna Ah Sam	University of Hawai'i at Mānoa
Michael Bamberger	Independent consultant
Gail Barrington	Barrington Research Group, Inc.
Fred Carden	International Development Research Centre
Thomas Chapel	Centers for Disease Control and Prevention
Leslie Cooksy	Sierra Health Foundation
Fiona Cram	Katoa Ltd.
Peter Dahler-Larsen	University of Southern Denmark
E. Jane Davidson	Real Evaluation Ltd.
Stewart Donaldson	Claremont Graduate University
Jody Fitzpatrick	University of Colorado Denver
Jennifer Greene	University of Illinois at Urbana-Champaign
Melvin Hall	Northern Arizona University
George M. Harrison	University of Hawai'i at Mānoa
Gary Henry	Vanderbilt University
Rodney Hopson	George Mason University
George Julnes	University of Baltimore
Jean King	University of Minnesota
Saville Kushner	University of Auckland
Robert Lahey	REL Solutions Inc.
Miri Levin-Rozalis	Ben Gurion University of the Negev and Davidson Institute at the Weizmann Institute of Science
Laura Leviton	Robert Wood Johnson Foundation
Melvin Mark	Pennsylvania State University
Sandra Mathison	University of British Columbia
Robin Lin Miller	Michigan State University
Michael Morris	University of New Haven
Debra Rog	Westat and the Rockville Institute
Patricia Rogers	Royal Melbourne Institute of Technology
Mary Ann Scheirer	Scheirer Consulting
Robert Schwarz	University of Toronto
Lyn Shulha	Queen's University
Nick L. Smith	Syracuse University
Sanjeev Sridharan	University of Toronto
Monica Stitt-Bergh	University of Hawai'i at Mānoa

Editorial Policy and Procedures

New Directions for Evaluation, a quarterly sourcebook, is an official publication of the American Evaluation Association. The journal publishes works on all aspects of evaluation, with an emphasis on presenting timely and thoughtful reflections on leading-edge issues of evaluation theory, practice, methods, the profession, and the organizational, cultural, and societal context within which evaluation occurs. Each issue of the journal is devoted to a single topic, with contributions solicited, organized, reviewed, and edited by one or more guest editors.

The editor-in-chief is seeking proposals for journal issues from around the globe about topics new to the journal (although topics discussed in the past can be revisited). A diversity of perspectives and creative bridges between evaluation and other disciplines, as well as chapters reporting original empirical research on evaluation, are encouraged. A wide range of topics and substantive domains is appropriate for publication, including evaluative endeavors other than program evaluation; however, the proposed topic must be of interest to a broad evaluation audience.

Journal issues may take any of several forms. Typically they are presented as a series of related chapters, but they might also be presented as a debate; an account, with critique and commentary, of an exemplary evaluation; a feature-length article followed by brief critical commentaries; or perhaps another form proposed by guest editors.

Submitted proposals must follow the format found via the Association's website at http://www.eval.org/Publications/NDE.asp. Proposals are sent to members of the journal's Editorial Advisory Board and to relevant substantive experts for single-blind peer review. The process may result in acceptance, a recommendation to revise and resubmit, or rejection. The journal does not consider or publish unsolicited single manuscripts.

Before submitting proposals, all parties are asked to contact the editor-in-chief, who is committed to working constructively with potential guest editors to help them develop acceptable proposals. For additional information about the journal, see the "Statement of the Editor-in-Chief" in the Spring 2013 issue (No. 137).

Paul R. Brandon, Editor-in-Chief
University of Hawai'i at Mānoa
College of Education
1776 University Avenue
Castle Memorial Hall, Rm. 118
Honolulu, HI 968222463
e-mail: nde@eval.org

CONTENTS

FROM THE EDITOR-IN-CHIEF

E valuation is receiving considerable attention this year. Under the leadership of EvalPartners, the collaborative endeavor of professional evaluation associations and organizations around the world, 2015 has been declared the International Year of Evaluation. A formal United Nations resolution has acknowledged this status, and associations are symbolically passing an evaluation torch from conference to conference.

In recognition of the current heightened attention to evaluation internationally, two issues of the journal this year will be presented by guest editors and authors, mostly from outside of North America. The present issue is edited by Barbara Rosenstein, Chairperson of the Israeli Association for Program Evaluation, and Helena Desivilya Syna, Chair of the MA Program in Organizational Development and Consulting at the Max Stern Yezreel Valley College in Israel. It is the first issue in the journal's 37-year history to focus mostly on evaluation in the Middle East, as well as the first since 1990 to focus on issues of social justice.

Dr. Rosenstein and Dr. Desivilya Syna state in the Editors' Notes that "the role of evaluation has expanded to include an almost 'watchdog' function of making sure that policy and programming protect the rights of all people and address issues affecting both marginalized and mainstream populations. Such a role is particularly important concerning programs and policies that do not refer to social justice explicitly." The reader will find much in this issue that supports this assertion.

Paul R. Brandon
Editor-in-Chief

NEW DIRECTIONS FOR EVALUATION, no. 146, Summer 2015   © 2015 Wiley Periodicals, Inc., and the American Evaluation Association.   Published online in Wiley Online Library (wileyonlinelibrary.com) • DOI: 10.1002/ev.20126

EDITORS' NOTES

M any significant changes have taken place in the theory and practice of evaluation in the last several decades. The issues of accountability and results-based programming were a major focus at the beginning of the 21st century, with random control trials taking center stage in the United States. Evaluation played a major role in contributing to these developments. However, the epistemology supporting the quantitative approach to evaluation was followed by concern for sustainability of "good" programs, greater use of mixed methods, and recognition of the complexity of both programs and evaluation (Bamberger & Vijayendra, 2010).

Alongside these changes in the field of evaluation, social scientists and evaluation practitioners became more aware of social justice and social responsibility due to socioeconomic and political transitions and their repercussions on social policies (Stuart, Grugulis, Tomlinson, Forde, & MacKenzie, 2013). These changes reflect widening gaps among social classes: the rich, the upper and lower middle classes, and the poor. The socioeconomic transformations are accompanied by vast reforms in the delivery of social services, which have swept the majority of the Western states. The most prominent change has been an application of market-type models to the provision of public services (Plantinga, de Ridder, & Corra, 2011). As a result of this transformation, the public sector has begun outsourcing social services to private and nongovernment organizations based on the premise that it would increase effectiveness and efficiency. Plantinga et al. cite research findings that seem to suggest that contracting out social services creates a quasi-market organizational environment, which in turn spurs competition and conflicting interests among various service providers. Such outcomes undermine equal opportunities and interfere with social justice. Thus, it is becoming increasingly necessary for those in positions of influence to join forces and take responsibility for promoting social justice. Evaluators are in a pivotal position to do so. Indeed, many of them are reemphasizing social justice and responsibility, as inspired by House's, Howe's, and Stake's frameworks (House & Howe, 1999; Stake, 2014). The current issue is on the forefront of this vanguard presenting a new direction: a pertinent and timely role of evaluation actively engaging social issues in the arena of increasing inequalities. We shed light on the evaluation–social justice interface in complex circumstances of conflict and social marginalization. Such an interface warrants special attention in a leading journal of the evaluation field.

NEW DIRECTIONS FOR EVALUATION, no. 146, Summer 2015   © 2015 Wiley Periodicals, Inc., and the American Evaluation Association.   Published online in Wiley Online Library (wileyonlinelibrary.com) • DOI: 10.1002/ev.20115

The Role of Evaluators in Promoting Social Justice

We draw on Rawls's (1999) conceptualization of social justice, usually labeled "justice as fairness." According to this scholar, social justice denotes ensuring and guarding equal access to civil freedoms, human rights, and opportunities, and protecting the least privileged members of society. Rawls's tenets concerning social justice refer to principles underlying the basic structures of society rather than principles that apply to institutions and associations in society or principles applying to international law. In this issue, we view social justice as a framework from which to address the evaluator's role in dealing with inequalities and power imbalance among social groups in society. Thus, in the field of evaluation, social responsibility is included in the concept of social justice.

In 2001, Mertens wrote: "the opportunity is upon us to engage in reciprocal learning and support, and to make a significant contribution to the amelioration of social and educational problems and the transformation of society to the end of greater justice and equality" (p. 373). Where are we now, almost 15 years after Mertens made her forecast? This issue of *New Directions for Evaluation* attempts to contribute to the fulfillment of that prophecy. Evaluators find themselves at the center of changing political agendas and in a position to influence these agendas by providing policy makers with evidence-based research to support and promote the merit and value of policy, programming, and project directions. We submit that the role of evaluation has expanded to include an almost "watchdog" function of making sure that policy and programming protect the rights of all people and address issues affecting both marginalized and mainstream populations. Such a role is particularly important concerning programs and policies that do not refer to *social justice* explicitly. Issues of inclusion and exclusion are implicit in all programming and we propose that it is the evaluator's role to ensure that these issues are placed firmly on the public agenda.

This issue reflects a *substantive focus*, honing in on this timely renewed role for evaluation from a variety of perspectives, stressing complex contexts that are characterized by social divisions among diverse social groups, as demonstrated in Israeli society. The main intricacies of such settings revolve around social divisions and intergroup tensions, features that accentuate the need to monitor social justice, especially as reflected in services provided to minorities and marginalized social groups.

The issue addresses these topics against the background of complex sociopolitical contexts attempting to answer the questions: How does the sociopolitical context foster or hinder more democratic and transformative evaluation approaches? And how does or can evaluation influence or have an impact on the sociopolitical context?

NEW DIRECTIONS FOR EVALUATION • DOI: 10.1002/ev

A range of evaluation approaches from responsive evaluation, democratic evaluation, social justice evaluation, as well as a variety of participatory forms of evaluation have proposed the social responsibility role of evaluation. These evaluations strive to give voice to the marginalized populations that are usually involved in a program or an intervention. Often, evaluators realize their increasing social responsibility through work in the field, reflect their understanding of the projects' participants and staff within their specific contexts and present an overview of society and societal needs to those in a position to make changes. In some instances they attempt to advocate change actively. The current issue explores the following topics related to evaluation in the pursuit of social justice and responsibility:

- The potential of evaluation to critique and transform the wider sociopolitical and socioeconomic context;
- Theoretical foundations and methodological approaches of this role of evaluation; and
- Possible ways whereby evaluation may promote social justice and responsibility for instance by implementing dialogical processes among stakeholders, especially in the context of asymmetric relationships, when strategic communication dominates and prevailing discourses silence certain voices.

In sum, the articles in this issue discuss (a) social justice methodologies in evaluation that use evaluation approaches which in and by themselves foster social justice; (b) evaluation use to promote social justice; and (c) evaluation of programs that emphasize social justice.

Brief Overview of the Articles

The articles in this issue concern various frequently marginalized social groups, exhibiting overt diversities as well as more hidden ones, such as national or ethnic minorities, women, and groups with special needs and disabilities. In many cases, the populations fit in several categories such as national minority women.

We have arranged the articles according to the population discussed in the article. Thus, the first two articles discuss issues related to evaluation, social responsibility, social justice, and marginalized populations in general. The third, fourth, and fifth articles address issues concerning populations marginalized due to health, psychological, and physical difficulties. The sixth, seventh, and eighth articles concern populations marginalized due to their cultural or ethnic/national status. And the final two articles confront issues involving the specific geopolitical context of the Israeli and Palestinian reality.

NEW DIRECTIONS FOR EVALUATION • DOI: 10.1002/ev

We begin with Woelders and Abma's discussion of an evaluation involving the marginalized population with disabilities in academia. The authors introduce Foucault's theory of normalization as a key to understanding social injustices and the role the evaluator can play in the process of using this theoretical framework. They discuss how a different perspective on "normal" can further inclusion. In the next article, Levin-Rozalis examines features of the evaluator's role that go beyond professional duties to conduct a good evaluation that meets professional standards, and answers these questions using Kant's categorical imperative, Ulrich's discussion on professionalism and systems, and Alexander's notion of a life worth living, among others. The third article addresses the issues of social space and social inclusion. Lapidot-Lefler, Friedman, Arieli, Haj, Sykes, and Kais demonstrate the need for new constructs to evaluate social inclusion and offer an innovative approach to programs involving disabled participants and their families. The article suggests that social space and field concepts can provide tools for generating "actionable" knowledge that can guide programs and practices aimed at inclusion. This article is followed by Desivilya Syna, Rottman, and Raz's illustration of a model used for promoting social justice in the increasingly competitive, insecure, and socially unjust field of employment. The proposed evaluation model draws on Abma and Widdershoven's (2008) typology concerning the relationship between evaluators and evaluees and is implemented in evaluation of a program attempting to integrate learning disabled college graduates in the labor market. In the fifth article, Gruskin, Waller, Safreed-Harmon, Ezer, Cohen, Gathumbi, and Kameri-Mbote present a mixed-methods model approach to assessing social justice aspects of evaluation in legalization of health programming. The authors show us a different setting, Kenya, demonstrating the global necessity to address the issues of social justice, responsibility in evaluation, and gender concerns with reference to vulnerable populations.

The six remaining articles provide case studies of the role of responsible evaluation in promoting social justice in a variety of settings in Israel and the Palestinian Authority. In the sixth article, Zamir and Abu Jaber discuss the ways in which evaluation pointed the Partner Development School program in a direction that included Bedouin women as teacher trainees. Through evaluation, cultural constraints that would have otherwise been ignored were incorporated into the program. Zoabi and Awad, in the seventh article, shine a new light on the role of evaluation in an affirmative action program within the framework of social justice and responsibility. Lustig, Ben Baruch-Koskas, Makhani-Belkin, and Hirsch present a dialog model of evaluation, focusing on a program with Ethiopian immigrants to Israel in the eighth article. The process promotes professional organizational discourse amongst several cycles, such as NGO commissioners, institute headquarters, the field practitioners, and the evaluation unit staff. In addition, the example illustrates how to build trust and partnership while turning organizational tacit knowledge into explicit knowledge. Bitar addresses the challenges of conducting a responsible, justice-oriented evaluation within a conflict setting in the ninth article. The article begins with a short history of the political situation and then examines and illustrates the impact of the Israeli occupation on the field of evaluation in the Occupied Palestinian Territories (oPt). More importantly, the article examines the role evaluators play in the oPt to promote social justice in the interventions that are taking place in the development arena and the challenges they face in so doing. The article concludes with the implications for and generalizability of the role of evaluators in promoting the social justice agenda in other conflict contexts. We conclude the issue with another discussion of the role of evaluation in a conflict setting. In the final article of the issue, Steinberg and Zamir tell the story of an Israeli–Palestinian partnership in constructing parallel narrative histories of the region and evaluation's contribution to this endeavor. This article opens a window revealing the challenging task of evaluating against the backdrop of complex, conflicting, and hostile interrelations.

It is important to mention that this issue of the journal is being prepared during the summer of 2014 at the height of the war in our region. These articles shine a ray of light into a seemingly dark intractable conflict. The discussion of narrative, challenges, hearing the voices of those who are rarely heard, and the possibility of working together adds a note of optimism at a generally pessimistic time.

References

Abma, T. A., & Widdershoven, G. A. M. (2008). Evaluation and/as social relation. *Evaluation, 14*(2), 209–225.

Bamberger, M., & Vijayendra, R. (2010). *Using mixed methods in monitoring and evaluation. Experiences from international development.* The World Bank Development Research Group Poverty and Inequality Team.

House, E. R., & Howe, K. R. (1999). *Values in evaluation and social research.* Thousand Oaks, CA: Sage.

Mertens, D. M. (2001). Inclusivity and transformation: Evaluation in 2010. *American Journal of Evaluation, 22*, 367–374.

Plantinga, M., de Ridder, K., & Corra, A. (2011). Choosing whether to buy or make: The contracting out of employment reintegration services by Dutch municipalities. *Social Policy and Administration, 45*(3), 245–263.

Rawls, J. (1999). *A theory of justice* (rev. ed.). Cambridge, MA: Belknap.

Stake, R. E. (2014). Eisner's qualities and quality. *American Journal of Evaluation, 35*, 453–454.

Stuart, M., Grugulis, I., Tomlinson, J., Forde, C., & MacKenzie, R. (2013). Reflections on work and employment into the 21st century: Between equal rights, force decides. *Work, Employment and Society, 27*(3), 379–395.

Barbara Rosenstein
Helena Desivilya Syna
Editors

BARBARA ROSENSTEIN *is a founding member and current chairperson of the Israeli Association for Program Evaluation. She was on the first board of the International Organization for Cooperation in Evaluation (IOCE), has taught evaluation theory and ethics, and currently conducts evaluations of social enterprise and social change programs.*

HELENA DESIVILYA SYNA *is a social/organizational psychologist and the current chair of the MA program in organizational development and consulting at the Max Stern Yezreel Valley College. Her areas of expertise, research, and publications revolve around social relations and social issues, especially management of social conflict, building partnerships, and intergroup collaborations.*

NEW DIRECTIONS FOR EVALUATION • DOI: 10.1002/ev

Woelders, S., & Abma, T. (2015). A different light on normalization: Critical theory and responsive evaluation studying social justice in participation practices. In B. Rosenstein & H. Desivilya Syna (Eds.), *Evaluation and social justice in complex sociopolitical contexts.* New Directions for Evaluation, 146, 9–18.

1

A Different Light on Normalization: Critical Theory and Responsive Evaluation Studying Social Justice in Participation Practices

Susan Woelders, Tineke Abma

Abstract

Responsive evaluation provides guidelines to include various stakeholders in dialogue. However, a substantial theory to understand power asymmetries and inequalities is lacking. The purpose of this article is to consider which theoretical framework for societal critique can be helpful to evaluate practices in relation to social justice. These questions will be addressed using fragments from a responsive evaluation study on the involvement of people with an intellectual disability in public policy. Our study shows that Foucault's framework on normalization was helpful. It revealed that the engagement and striving for equality and social justice can turn out to be disciplining itself. © 2015 Wiley Periodicals, Inc., and the American Evaluation Association.

Social justice has been explicitly addressed as a concern in the evaluation literature (Greene, 2006; Mertens, 2009; Schwandt, 1997). Responsive evaluation is an approach that aims to enhance the mutual understanding between stakeholder groups and value-driven transformations (Abma, 2005; Abma & Widdershoven, 2011; Guba & Lincoln, 1989). Responsive evaluation takes into account the issues and voices of as many stakeholders as possible, as well as those who are less heard in policymaking. It is an interactive, reflexive process on the meanings and values of a practice with and among all groups whose interests are involved. This is stimulated by dialogue between the different stakeholder groups. Dialogue is a learning process oriented toward mutual understanding (versus a debate focused on strategic action). In dialogue, people meet each other as persons with a name and face (and not as parties in a debate).

In responsive evaluation, the evaluator should create a power balance between the various stakeholders, leveling power differentials among groups. The empowerment of marginalized groups is in some sense an extension of this (Baur & Abma, 2011; Mertens, 2009). To level out the influence of all stakeholders, most of the time it is necessary to support the weaker voices. In the absence of the evaluator's advocacy for minority group interests, majority elite views can dominate (House, 1993).

Methodologically, responsive evaluation provides guidelines to include various stakeholders and to reckon with power differentials. Stakeholder groups are first consulted separately; a phase of collaboration and dialogue to share stakeholder issues then follows. The evaluator acts as an interpreter of stakeholder issues, a process facilitator for the dialogue, an educator to foster mutual understanding, and a Socratic guide who evokes reflection on taken-for-granted issues. However, there is no substantial theory to elucidate power asymmetries and inequalities. Critical theory can be helpful in interpreting power issues and in shining a light on social justice in the practice that is evaluated.

We draw on Foucault (1982, 1984, 1989, 1997) to explicate power issues. Foucault maintained that economic and political demands dominate in today's society. These demands dominate people through discipline and principles of *normalization*. The goal of this discipline is to make citizens politically obedient and economically productive. Norms are embedded in discourses, and these discourses reflect and reestablish hierarchies in societies. Power issues are at stake here. Indeed, when people do not meet the ideal norms, they are excluded. Foucault argued that it is important to unravel these processes of normalization, because defining the norm leads to processes of inclusion and exclusion. Power issues in organizations can be studied from this point of view in order to shed light on social justice.

Method

The focus of the presented responsive evaluation was the participation of people with intellectual disability (ID) in policy-making, education and research. In this project, which took place over 18 months in the Netherlands, we wanted to know the conditions necessary for people with ID to participate and how the environment can be more open and inclusive to allow the voices of people with ID to be heard.

NEW DIRECTIONS FOR EVALUATION • DOI: 10.1002/ev

To find answers to these questions, we selected three different participation practices in which people with ID already participate. One of the practices involved was the participation of people with ID in policy making in client councils of a health care organization: De Regenboog (the name is a pseudonym). This practice is the focus of this article because it provides a good case for learning and shows our use of critical theory to interpret participation practices.

The responsive evaluation approach was chosen to increase the personal and mutual understanding of the particular situation of participation. Therefore, we included as many stakeholders as possible: people with ID and coaches, managers, and parents of people with ID from the health care organization. Evaluation activities included interviews (structured and open), participant observations, and focus groups. We interviewed 10 clients with ID who participate in the client councils, two parents of clients with ID, six coaches and two managers. Topics included experiences of members in the client councils, the meaning of participation in the councils, and having a voice. Participant observations included six client council meetings. In the collaboration phase, one focus group was held with all the coaches at De Regenboog. Finally, one mixed focus group was organized with professionals and clients that included participants from the three evaluation sites. An inductive thematic analysis revealed the issues of the various stakeholder groups. In a secondary analysis, these issues were related to the framework of Foucault.

We were aware of the power imbalance between the stakeholders, and wanted to give voice to those in a more vulnerable situation—in this case, the people with ID, who were care dependent. We decided to work together with people with ID in our own evaluation team. Including people with ID meant they could bring in their own experiential knowledge, and hierarchic relations between evaluators and researched could be redressed (Nierse & Abma, 2011; Oliver, 1992). They could also relate to other people with ID and make it easier to gain access to the practices and people we wanted to contact and talk to.

From Theory to Practice: Setting

De Regenboog is an organization in the Netherlands that provides care and support to 2,200 people with ID, as well as to their parents. De Regenboog values the involvement of clients with ID in their organization. Besides normative arguments of rights and justice (clients must be able to have a say and raise their voice), the organization has to meet legal demands concerning client councils. Since 1996, the involvement of clients in care organizations is supported by law in the Netherlands (this law is named Wet Medezeggenschap Cliënten Zorgsector). This law is based on the idea that the daily experiences of clients should inform the board of directors of care institutions and that decisions of the board should match client input. In this way, clients have a say in decisions that influence their lives.

In Regenboog, clients in a council regularly gather to discuss a variety of issues. Issues can be brought up by management, because legally they have to get advice from the client council about certain policy issues (such as safety plans, food, and year plans). Clients can also bring in issues to discuss.

Clients get support to learn to fulfill their role in the client council. The organization also developed supporting material to structure the meeting, like a guideline with pictograms and a gavel for the chairman. One of the clients fulfills the function of the chairman and notes are made. This structure gives support to the clients. They know what to do in which order, and the materials are accessible and understandable for them. In a constructive way, the organization has tried to make the formal framework of a meeting accessible for people with ID.

Clients are also supported by a coach (a professional from De Regenboog). The coach can help with practical issues such as making notes, getting into contact with managers, and helping to supply transport for clients between locations. In addition, coaches try to make issues and policy understandable for clients. They also help the client council determine their position in relation to the questions about policy measures that are submitted to them from management. Finally, the coach also monitors the structure of the meetings.

Findings

Clients

The clients who participate in the client councils value their roles. Being a member of the client council means taking on a social role, and it is a way to open up their horizons. It feels good for them to be part of a group, and participation gives them the opportunity to learn new skills. The value for the clients lies mostly in the participation itself and feelings of "belonging." A client council member explained:

> The client council, what I do … Just attending the meeting and talking. I'm not there on my own; we are with four or five of us. I mainly do it to attend and be there. (Member)

Client council members do not explicitly express the value of having a say or having a voice and influence on decision-making processes in the organization. Some of them—mainly clients who have been in the client council for a longer time—do value the fact that they can express themselves and voice concerns of other clients.

> I think it's important to speak up for the ones who live here. It means that I have a say and that I can help to decide. It's important to speak up in the group. You have to make clear what you want. (Member)

NEW DIRECTIONS FOR EVALUATION • DOI: 10.1002/ev

They value the supporting materials, and all clients think that the support of the coach is essential; they cannot do the job without their help.

> Without the coach it will be a mess. We could not have this meeting without the coach. We wouldn't know where to start and who would make the notes? (Member)

But the coaches are not only important for the structure during the meeting; they also help to interpret what a client member brings in:

> The coach has to understand us. When one of us cannot express what he means, the coach can explain what he means. (Member)

Coaches

To enable the participation of clients in the client council, the role of the coach is crucial. As expressed by the clients, coaches create structure. In fact the coach builds a bridge between the management of the organization and the clients.

In practice, the coaches feel tension. They have to make issues accessible and understandable for clients, but they do not want to guide them too much. The line between enabling clients to make up their own mind and influencing them sometimes feels blurred. A coach:

> Sometimes I see that people do exactly what you bring up. In fact you have to help them to structure and give them a framework otherwise you have nothing. That's really a tightrope.

Another coach also expresses the tension she experiences:

> They want to be treated in a certain way, like adults and they don't want to be carried on the hand. But abstract issues are very difficult to understand. Because abstract thinking, that's difficult for them, at least, that's part of their disability. Finding this balance is sometimes difficult.

Manager of Client Participation

The manager of client participation states that the participation of people with ID has undergone tremendous development. She refers to the situation where people with ID were locked away in institutions and their disability was a taboo for society:

> While in the past they didn't have a voice and were not involved, today opportunities are created to make it possible to participate and to raise their voice. This development has been a struggle and it still goes on.

She is proud of what is made possible in the organization. People with ID are involved at diverse levels. Both the managers and the board of the organization value this participation. From her perspective, participation is not just organizing and giving instruments for involvement; it is about "the input of the other person, about the meeting of person to person." This makes involvement an ethical issue relating to the realm of proximity between self and other. She refers to this as a "precarious process" that is under pressure in times of financial cuts.

First Analysis and Reflection

Looking at the practice of involving people with ID in the client councils, one could argue that all formal requirements for a client council are met. More than that, the councils are actively supported. Time and money are spent on this, and an effort is made to make the councils accessible to clients and clients accessible to the councils. Clients value their role; it offers them new opportunities and broadens their horizons. The question is whether this approach leaves enough room for the experiences of the clients themselves and the values in their lives. The issues that are discussed in the councils can be very abstract and hard to understand and reflect on. The coaches experience tension: They support the clients to make up their minds and to formulate answers to policy questions. At the same time, they do not want to be too decisive. They have to discuss certain policy issues due to legal demands, but these issues can be very difficult.

When we look at the fulfillment of the chairman role, we see that the guidance of the coach is needed. In fact, the coach structures the meeting and coordinates all activities. The role of the chairman becomes a symbolic one. This is a complicated issue, because the people with ID who fulfill this role are proud to be able to do so. They feel recognized. The meeting minutes play an important role during the meetings. It takes a lot of time to go through the paperwork, and not everybody receives the minutes before the meeting. Some clients need the support of staff to read and understand the notes. It seems that the notes fit the formal framework, but that in practice the value of the content is insignificant or even symbolic.

Tension is also experienced by the evaluators themselves, as expressed in their field notes and reflection sessions:

> I'm impressed by what I have seen during my observations in the client council of De Regenboog. A lot of effort is made to let people with ID participate in the councils and involve them in policy. And I can see that the people with ID value what they do. It's important for them. And yet, afterwards I feel uncomfortable. Why do I have the feeling that no justice is done to people with ID? I recognized this discomfort in the book of a philosopher and mother with a son, Ramon, with Down syndrome, who wrote:

"Ramon is not a client council member. He cannot talk. But two of his friends are client council members. They can say 'yes' and 'no.' What they agree with is considered to be the outcome of a 'democratic decision-making process.' A lot of organizations correctly comply with policy that is based on autonomy as a general ideal for all" (Rondhuis, 2011, p. 91).

How does this all relate to what I see and experience? (Evaluator, the first author). "Your critical question stemming from uncomfortable feelings is situated in your body at that moment. You still haven't words to analyze the situation. Yet, you acknowledge that these feelings and experiences have a right of their own and can function as a compass to search for different interpretations of what is going on in the studied practice" (Evaluator, the second author).

Dialogue

The findings were difficult to discuss with the coaches, the coordinator of the department for client participation, and the manager of client participation. Although they were open to feedback, admitting the fact that people with ID have their limitations is a sensitive issue. Coaches deny feelings of tension or struggle and only make an effort to think about new ways to approach the involvement of clients with ID.

Taking a Closer Look: Secondary Analysis Through the Lens of Foucault

Foucault argued that in today's society there are informal, unwritten rules—the norms to which people have to conform in order to meet goals for political obedience and economic productivity. On the one hand, this leads to homogenization (everybody has to meet the same demands); on the other hand, it leads to exclusion. After all, not everybody complies with the unwritten standards and norms. According to Foucault, disciplining power created differences and hierarchies and processes of inclusion and exclusion.

Inclusion and exclusion are also highly debated themes in the field of disability studies (DS). An important aim of DS is to contribute to more social justice and equal rights for people with disabilities (Vehmas & Watson, 2014; Young & Quibell, 2000). Disabled people should have the same rights and obligations as other citizens. The viewpoint of DS is that disability is socially constructed, which means that it is the result of the way society deals with disabilities. People with disabilities are like everybody else. Society itself makes the difference. When society is more open and inclusive to people with disabilities, inequalities can be eliminated and social justice can be achieved. Aiming for normalization and social role valorization can contribute to this process.

New Directions for Evaluation • DOI: 10.1002/ev

In line with this thinking of the disability movement, professionals, family members and advocates of people with ID in De Regenboog take normalization of people with ID as a starting point to strive for more equality and social justice. From their point of view, the recognition of differences and disability is at odds with this striving for normalization. Making differences explicit leads to inequality and social injustice. In line with the disability movement, the organization has to include people with ID. It is up to society (that is, the organization) to be inclusive, make an effort to help people take on new social roles, and empower them. The societal norm that everyone has to be autonomous is not put under scrutiny.

However, Foucault argued that normalization is a way to discipline people. This discipline is a form of power to ensure that people meet the standards of what is "normal" in our practice; people with ID have to function as autonomous persons who are able to raise their voices and can form their opinions about policy issues (see McIntosh, 2002). Although coaches struggle with this norm in their work with people with ID, the difference (not being able to fulfill the norm) is not acknowledged. It is *not done* to recognize inabilities. But it is exactly this denying of difference that can lead to exclusion and social injustice, from the point of view of Foucault. Striving for normalization turns out to be an excluding process.

> It is exactly this viewpoint of Foucault that enables me to interpret my feelings of discomfort when I observed the meeting of the client council. No effort is too much for the organisation to make it possible for people with ID to participate in the client council. But in order to achieve their involvement, people with ID have to fit in the formal framework of a client council meeting. They have to comply with the liberal norm of the free and autonomous individual who operates without help of others. From my point of view it is exactly this striving for normalization that does no justice to them. They are not valued for the unique persons they are. (Evaluator)

Conclusion

In this article, we have shown how responsive evaluation can be helpful to study social justice. The methodology itself tries to overcome imbalance of power by including various stakeholders and by giving voice to marginalized voices and groups. By doing so, responsive evaluation offers the possibility to map the meaning and values of all stakeholders concerning the issues under study. This is not only about facts, but about the stories of the people involved, and the values that are of interest to them.

As we have shown in our research in the participation practice, a lot of effort was made to involve people with ID in the client councils. But still there were unsettling feelings and observations that justice was not done to people with ID in the studied participation practices. These embodied experiences of the evaluator were taken seriously and encouraged us to search hidden norms. Applying the theory of Foucault provided us with the opportunity to better understand our own unsettling feelings and the practice under study.

Foucault's theory illuminated the disciplining effects of normalization and the limitations of rational communication. Together, these concepts complemented our understanding of social injustices in the participation practices of people with ID. These imbalances of power do not disappear easily. The evaluator can bring these power issues to the surface, and this may evoke and broaden the dialogue as new understandings brought up. Then it is up to the people involved to change the status quo. This requires an open mind to understand others' viewpoints, and a close look at one's own values (Abma & Widdershoven, 2011).

Reflection is also an important activity of the evaluator. Especially important is the recognition of the value of bodily resistance as a compass to search for new understandings of social justice and injustice. Based on such reflections, the evaluator can bring in the unrevealed processes of power and use the dis-ability to trouble societal norms and disciplining practices (Goodley & Runswick-Cole, 2014). to enrich and broaden the dialogue and mutual understanding.

References

Abma, T. A. (2005). Responsive evaluation: Its meaning and special contribution to health promotion. *Evaluation and Program Planning, 28,* 279–289.

Abma T. A., & Widdershoven, G. A. (2011). Evaluation as a relationally responsive practice. In N. K. Denzin & Y. S. Lincoln (Eds.), *The Sage handbook of qualitative research* (pp. 669–680). Los Angeles, CA: Sage.

Baur, V. E., & Abma, T. A. (2011). Resident councils between lifeworld and system: Is there room for communicative action? *Journal of Aging Studies, 25*(4), 390–396.

Foucault, M. (1982). The subject and power. *Critical Inquiry, 8*(4), 777–795.

Foucault, M. (1984). What is enlightenment? In P. Rabinow (Ed.), *The Foucault reader* (pp. 32–50). New York, NY: Pantheon.

Foucault, M. (1989). *Discipline, toezicht en straf—de geboorte van de gevangenis.* Groningen: Historische Uitgeverij.

Foucault, M. (1997). *Essential works: 1954–1984. Ethics: Subjectivity and truth.* New York, NY: New Press.

Goodley, D., & Runswick-Cole, K. (2014). Becoming dishuman: Thinking about the human through dis/ability. *Studies in the Cultural Politics of Education.* doi: 10.1080/01596306.2014.930021

Greene, J. C. (2006). Evaluation, democracy and social change. In I. F. Shaw, J. C. Greene, & M. M. Marks (Eds,), *The Sage handbook of evaluation* (pp. 141–160). London, England: Sage.

Guba, E. G., & Lincoln, Y. S. (1989). *Fourth generation evaluation.* Beverly Hills, CA: Sage

House, E. R. (1993). *Professional evaluation.* Beverly Hills, CA: Sage.

McIntosh, P. (2002). An archi-texture of learning disability services: The use of Michel Foucault. *Disability & Society, 17*(1), 65–79.

Mertens, D. (2009). *Transformative research and evaluation.* New York, NY: Guilford.

Nierse, C. J., & Abma, T. A. (2011). Developing voice and empowerment: The first step towards a broad consultation in research agenda setting. *Journal of Intellectual Disability Research*, 55(4), 411–421.

Oliver, M. (1992). Changing the social relations of research production. *Disability, Handicap and Society*, 7(2), 101–114.

Rondhuis, T. (2011). *De mongool, de moeder en de filosoof*. Utrecht: Uitgeverij Ten Have.

Schwandt, T. S. (1997). Whose interests are being served? Program evaluation as conceptual practice of power. In L. Mabry (Ed.), *Evaluation and the post-modern dilemma: Advances in program evaluation* (Vol. 3, pp. 89–104). Greenwich, CT: JAI.

Vehmas, S., & Watson, N. (2014). Moral wrongs, disadvantages and disability: A critique of critical disability studies. *Disability & Society*, 29(4), 638–650.

Young, D. A., & Quibell, R. (2000). Why rights are never enough: Rights, intellectual disability and understanding. *Disability & Society*, 15(5), 747–764.

Susan Woelders is a junior researcher at the Department of Medical Humanities, VU University Medical Centre, and the EMGO+ Research Institute for Health and Care Research, Amsterdam, The Netherlands.

Tineke Abma is a professor of participation and diversity at the Department of Medical Humanities, VU University Medical Centre, and a research leader in the EMGO+ Research Institute for Health and Care Research, Amsterdam, The Netherlands.

Levin-Rozalis, M. (2015). A purpose-driven action: The ethical aspect and social responsibility of evaluation. In B. Rosenstein & H. Desivilya Syna (Eds.), *Evaluation and social justice in complex sociopolitical contexts. New Directions for Evaluation, 146*, 19–32.

2

A Purpose-Driven Action: The Ethical Aspect and Social Responsibility of Evaluation

Miri Levin-Rozalis

Abstract

This article raises questions concerning the boundaries of the evaluator's role and the scope of evaluation with regard to ethical issues. In a unique dialog format, a variety of thinkers are brought to the stage in order to illuminate these issues. Their collective answer is that evaluators bear a very great social responsibility: to look broadly, to look forward, to be responsible for their actions, and as far as possible, to be sure that their efforts are indeed for the benefit of those who will ultimately be affected by their work. © 2015 Wiley Periodicals, Inc., and the American Evaluation Association.

The American Evaluation Association (AEA) conference always makes my head spin: thousands of people running from hall to hall, hundreds of sessions discussing an infinite number of subjects, the sound of masses of people walking, talking, meeting, looking around, seeking a familiar face or immersed in the program and trying to find the hall they want to get to. Amid this tumult I heard a man's voice call my name.

This article is a shortened version of Chapter 9 in Levin-Rozalis, M. (2014). Let's talk program evaluation in theory and practice. CA: Samuel Wachtman's Sons, Inc. http://www.amazon.com/Program-Evaluation-Theory-Practice-Lets/dp/1888820632

"It's been a long time," he said loudly, trying to speak over the din. "Shall we get away from the noise?" he shouted. "It's a lovely day outside."

And so I found myself sitting opposite him on a café veranda on Baltimore's beautiful waterfront.

"I've got a problem that's worrying me," he said. "I've just completed a comprehensive evaluation in conjunction with a government ministry, involving activities with migrants. The ministry is investing a great deal of money, energy, and goodwill, and in the short term, they're improving things—the program is working well in the framework of its rationale and goals, it's meeting the schedule, it's within budget, and it's reaching its planned goals in the best possible way. The problem is that I feel this is done at the expense of the community and family infrastructure. The program staff is building up a young, educated, modern leadership, one that's easier for the authorities to live with, while shunting aside the traditional leadership. Their point of departure is that it's for the community's benefit: The young leadership will lead it toward better integration into the general population. But I think that these young, educated guys can't lead the mainly traditional community. And what will happen is that they will be integrated into the general population, while the majority of the not-well-educated community will be unable to follow them. And since the traditional leadership is being eased out as a result of the intervention, and the strong younger people are leaving, what will remain is a weakened, alienated, headless community that can't find its way. And that, I fear, is a long-lasting tragedy. I'm afraid that such a community will provide endless work for a long line of social workers, perhaps even the police, not to mention the vacuum that will allow various kinds of radicals to fill."

"And you are deliberating over the extent to which you, as a *professional*, have the right to push your own worldview at the expense of that of the intervention."

"Yes. I'm asking about the evaluator's boundaries as a professional. And moreover, I'm asking a moral question about the evaluator's right, or even duty to intervene in matters that aren't part of his job description."

"We've learned that evaluation is judgmental," I said, "because it gives value to the things it evaluates. But we've also learned—with great emphasis—that as evaluators, we're not allowed to be judgmental. We can't allow our personal judgment to bias the evaluation."

"That's precisely what I'm asking: first, about my right, as a professional, not a private individual, to judge—allowing my biases or inclinations or values to lead my considerations; also about my criteria for valuing my own judgment over the judgment of others."

"At the first conference on evaluation I attended many years ago, somebody stood up and spoke about the unholy alliance between evaluators and program operators or their funding bodies. He contended that, by the very fact that evaluators examine a program's inner workings and not its broader context, they form that alliance. His words have remained with me since then, and I always try to examine which unholy alliance I'm serving."

"It's quite similar," he said sadly. "If I keep quiet, I really am forming an unholy alliance with the intervention, and I feel bad about it. If I speak out, I'm exceeding my authority as an evaluator. Perhaps they're right in what they're doing, and there's no alternative but to break up the traditional community."

"So you're also asking whether, as an evaluator, *you have the right* to judge the intervention's goals."

"You're right in part. Evaluation usually examines internal goals, which creates the unholy alliance you're talking about. It sometimes examines the quality of those goals, too. I'm not talking about judging the goals in the technical sense, judgment that asks to what extent they're clear and exhaustive, and to what extent they express the actual endeavor. But about judgment of their essence: their contribution to the evaluees, the community, and society."

"You're also asking about judging the fundamental value of the goals. Do the intervention program's goals see the entire community or just the specific target population? Do the goals cover a sufficiently long period?"

"Yes, I believe that if the intervention people had looked at the entire community, it should have appeared in their goals, or at least, in the rationale."

"Let's summarize the questions that you've raised up to now," I said, "so that we don't get lost. The first is, what are the boundaries of the evaluator's role (or, in other words, what is the evaluator's professional responsibility)? The second is, how broadly and how far should the intervention people, and especially the evaluator, look (whether to examine only the program or also the context)? And the third question is, does the evaluator have the right to judge (or evaluate) the intervention's goals?"

"Right. And I want to examine the goals with regards to a worldview, not just their technical merits."

"Look, if you're asking about judging the goals, then Friedman and his colleagues (2006) addressed that issue, but more in the direction of the fourth generation. They speak about the emergence of the different worldviews held by a program's stakeholders. They did this in order to create understanding and agreement between the partners. But you're going even further and asking how you choose between these worldviews. How do we build a professional compass, something that can tell us what's good and what's bad? And that's perhaps the most important question, because it also dictates the breadth of the picture we'll look at as evaluators. So your fourth question is: What is the role of your worldview versus that of the intervention people in the evaluation process? Or in other words, what compass does the evaluator have to sufficiently answer these questions?" I said.

"You've put it in a nutshell," he smiled.

"Many serious questions?"

"Yes," he nodded soberly. "All these questions are causing a commotion together in my mind. It's as if the more I know, the more experience I have, the more difficult the decisions become, because the questions become more difficult too."

"Werner Ulrich (2001) addressed expertise and has a very interesting approach to it."

"Enlighten me," he said.

"I hope I can. Ulrich contends that expertise isn't the high road to confidence, but the opposite. Expertise is more a matter of questions rather than answers. He also contends that expertise expands, and with that expansion, the responsibility of the expert expands correspondingly on several levels. First, the expert must recognize that it is not humanly possible to discuss all the aspects of a problem."

"But we still labor under the delusion that if we choose the questions and means of testing correctly, we'll obtain a correct answer. But correct according to what? According to whom? According to which criteria?"

"That's just it, there are no answers to those questions, at least according to Ulrich," I said. "One of the problems with making any decision and choosing any methodology is selectivity."

"Which means?"

"That something always remains outside our field of vision. And what we must take into account is what remains outside. What we're losing by following our choice, not what we're gaining. Qualitative methods, for instance, leave the distribution and power of the findings outside, whereas with quantitative methods it's the variety. But even without the methodology's limitations, any focus on one specific question bypasses what wasn't asked."

"Well, that's certainly thought-provoking."

"And more important," I went on, "an expert must know how to identify the questions that she or her methodology can't answer. That's the difference between an expert and a technician. Experts have to constantly observe themselves and test whether the path they've chosen is the best one in the existing circumstances—the best in the sense that it gives them reliable answers."

"It's a real paradox," my colleague said with frustration. "The more expertise expands, the more do the responsibility and the doubts. And as evaluators, our doubts are about everything: our basic assumptions, our questions, work procedures, the findings and how we interpret them, and how we derive recommendations for action from them."

"There's no rest for the wicked," I said with a wicked smile.

"There isn't, or answers either, because this whole discussion of ours still hasn't shown me a good way of knowing what to do."

"I suppose it does make things more difficult, rather than helping," I agreed. "Being a technician is far easier than being an expert."

"Now she tells me."

"Ulrich further contends that, even when the aim of evaluation is to test whether a specific work method is successful, the subjects of the evaluation are people, and the findings and recommendations are addressed to people. Therefore, there's social significance in what we do as evaluators."

"Right, that's where we started," he said with a sigh.

"Okay," I went on. "On the question of whether a program is successful, Ulrich suggests answering the question 'What is improvement?' in a complex manner, particularly while understanding our own values, which define what improvement is for us, and also in connection with the groups of people likely to be influenced by the evaluation process or its attendant side effects. And they're not only the evaluation clients."

"It sounds like fourth-generation evaluation."

"Not really. He doesn't talk about joint construction of a worldview. He addresses the evaluator's sphere of responsibility, and it's up to evaluators to declare which and whose values their evaluation promotes. He opposes the frequently heard argument that professional evaluation serves all interests equally."

"But he does introduce into the equation anybody who's involved in the process in one way or another."

"Yes, but into the evaluator's equation. Ulrich argues that the evaluator's vision of what change the evaluation needs to create and in whom must be constantly examined. And evaluators must examine their own vision. According to Ulrich, reflection such as these drive the professional thinking process forward more than any other point of observation."

"For years, we've been taught about scientific objectivity, about this separation of powers—we can't allow our personal inclinations, opinions, and beliefs to dictate the outcome of our evaluation."

"And now," I said with a smile, "your definition of yourself as an expert obliges you to consider your own beliefs and values. Because, as experts, the questions we must ask ourselves are not only how to conduct a good evaluation, or which methodology to use, but to what end we're conducting it, and who and what this evaluation serves, and also who and what we want it to serve. That's what Ulrich contends."

"Well, if the question is 'to what end,' that means that our prime concern is the character and implications of the evaluation results, and not the methodology used," he said, somewhat depressed.

"And that's only part of it!" I exclaimed. "Since evaluation is purpose-driven, it's teleological. It has direction because it's done in order to reach a result."

"And as you're always saying, research seeks reasons for phenomena; that's its purpose. Evaluation uses the reasons for a purpose, to create a result about a concrete object."

"Absolutely," I agreed, "and a generally accepted evaluation result is, for instance, to help the person who commissioned the evaluation to make practical decisions about the evaluation objects."

"And also," my friend continued, brightening up, "research has a subject but evaluation has objects. And since the object of the evaluation always relates to people's actions, there's no way of avoiding a discussion—not only on professional questions—but also on the ethical questions that brings me back to the question of the compass."

"Well, right now I've got three different lines of thought on responses to your questions."

"Three's fine," he laughed. "It's a number I can deal with. What are they?"

"On the question of the compass, the first that comes to mind is Kant's (1991) categorical imperative which provides a partial answer."

"And what about the legitimacy of my worldview?"

"On that, Professor Hanan Alexander (2006) provides a certain answer with his 'a life that is worth living' concept. And on the question of the broad canvas, we'll go back to Ulrich (2001) and Churchman (1968a, 1968b), and I hope that all of them will come together in a concept of a fifth generation of evaluation as I understand it, a concept that will perhaps provide an answer to all your questions."

My colleague smiled. "Fine, let's decipher them one by one."

"Shall we begin with Kant?"

"Let's," he agreed. "Kant held a clear and determined position: 'Act in such a way that you always treat humanity, whether in your own person or in the person of any other, never merely as a means to an end, but always at the same time as an end' (1991)," he declaimed with pathos.

"Indeed, and the research objects in evaluation are people. Always. Even when the evaluation's objective is to examine whether a work method is successful," I said.

"But Kant bothers me less," my colleague said. "He was a deontologist. That is, he contended that ethical considerations and moral laws should guide our behavior regardless of its outcome, and that we must behave in accordance with universal moral principles such as honesty, fairness, human rights, justice, and respect for others. I conscientiously behave that way, so Kant doesn't influence the methodology I choose."

"Perhaps not the methodology. The relationship with the evaluees is always a means. It's never a purpose in and of itself. There are evaluation approaches that attempt to bypass this: empowerment evaluation, democratic evaluation, participatory evaluation and constructivist evaluation (Cousins & Whitmore, 1998; Fetterman, 1994; Greene, 2000; Guba & Lincoln, 1989). Although all these approaches allow lots of room for the evaluees, and the evaluees are likely to gain from the interaction with the evaluation, they are still not the evaluation's purpose. They're a means for creating the knowledge that the evaluation needs, that the intervention people need. I've attempted to deal with this problem with my cybernetic approach (Levin-Rozalis, 2010)."

"We've crashed at the first of your three lines of thought," my colleague said, frowning.

"I'm not sure we have. Perhaps we should go a little deeper into Kant's words."

"Enlighten me."

"Dr. Niva Arav (2010), for instance, contends that at the basis of Kant's categorical imperative lies the principle of freedom of action. Kant states that humans are free creatures, and freedom, in his opinion, is manifested in our ability to think about our behavior and our ability to change that behavior in a way that meets our needs."

"Meaning," he said enthusiastically, "that all the participatory approaches you mentioned, which give the evaluees tools and knowledge that extend their range of choices, clearly meet the criterion of Kant's categorical imperative."

"They do," I replied, "because Kant contends that freedom of action is dependent on knowledge, and if we expand the evaluees' knowledge and allow them to choose, then there's evidently no problem. There is, however, a big problem in an action that prevents the evaluees from setting their goals for themselves."

"Then the question reverts to the intervention program itself," he remarked thoughtfully. "Doesn't the intervention program prevent the participants from setting goals for themselves and deciding about events of which they are a part?"

"A good question. According to Kant, as I understand him, that's something that evaluation should examine."

"We're getting into an infinite loop," he said, shaking his head, "because, as interveners or evaluators, we have no ability to do anything at all. Any decision we make, even a decision to teach people and give them the tools for making a better choice, is one we've made for somebody else."

"You're right," I replied. "But it seems that Kant gave us an answer to that with his principle of universality, with his contention that every moral law or principle must be universal, in the sense of being suitable for everyone. And that's conditional upon a positive answer to the question of whether I'd want everyone to act like me, or act toward me as I act."

"That also means," he went on, "that we must be prepared for the choice made by the evaluees to be a choice that runs counter to our worldview, values, or wishes. And that seems to be against human nature."

"It's certainly against the nature of the various do-gooders," I laughed.

"And what does all that say about my present quandary?" he asked.

"It raises questions," I replied. "First, about the community and the choices it can or can't make in the intervention framework."

"Yes, but that's less important for me," he said pensively.

"But still," I persisted, "from the intervention's standpoint, it's important to examine whether it has extended or narrowed the community's ability to choose. That can be your important contribution to the community, to place—as a criterion for a good evaluation—extending their possibilities of choice."

"I'm not sure how intervention can narrow it. After all, in our world at least we intervene in order to do good."

"I'll give you an example. At one of the international conferences on evaluation, an evaluator spoke about a project she evaluated in Egypt. The project set up a purified running-water system for a series of villages. Although the water reached the houses, the village women continued the traditional way of walking a long way to a well, drawing water, and carrying the heavy cans of water home on their head."

"Why?"

"The evaluator examined this and found that, for the women, walking to the well together was the only social interaction they had outside the family and one of the few possibilities they had of getting out of the house and away from their interminable household tasks."

"But going back to my problem, Kant is in fact telling me that my opinion on what's right or not right for the community isn't important as long as the principle of universality is maintained. What the community thinks about itself is important. But then what? Not to pipe running water to it? After all, isn't the right to purified water as universal as the women's right to social interaction outside their four walls?"

I looked at him, unsure about what to say. It seemed that the question was becoming increasingly complicated. "It looks like we need to think up a third solution, or a series of solutions whereby the lion's hunger is satisfied but the sheep remains whole."

"Such as?"

"I don't know. Maybe by separating the water into drinking water in the faucets, and water for household use, from the well that would compel the women to walk to it. Am I a water engineer?"

"Okay, okay," he said, holding up his hands. "So what Kant in fact contributes to my question of a compass that I can use to examine my worldview with regard to that of the intervention people is the issue of extending the evaluees' possibilities of choice, and the issue of universality. Two things that aren't easy to examine with a slide rule in complex situations. Sometimes one thing comes at the expense of the other." He paused. "It's reasonable to assume that the program I'm evaluating is extending the possibilities of choice for the young leadership it's fostering at the expense of the traditional leadership, and also at the expense of the community's weaker parts, which remain without their own talented young leadership."

"It's true that it isn't easy," I agreed. "Maybe what we need to do here is to draw attention to the weakening of the community and suggest to the intervention people that they seek a third way, one that will keep the young leadership in the community."

"I don't know. How do you do that without manipulation?"

"Perhaps by examining the life that the community sees as worth living?"

"Fine. So tell me about Professor Alexander and life that's worth living."

"Alexander (2006) speaks about educational research, but what he has to say is very appropriate for evaluation. He contends that a researcher must have a unique viewpoint stemming from a subjective perception of reality."

"The researcher?" he asked.

"Mainly the researcher or evaluator who is responsible for the implications of the research. They don't work in a vacuum."

"But we were taught that our responsibility is solely to rigorously and responsibly conduct worthy research, and that the results of such a research process have a life that's detached from the researcher—as though research conducted in an appropriate manner creates a truth that's beyond any consideration of the researcher."

"And that's why Alexander talks about 'a view from somewhere': a subject- or context-dependent viewpoint. And he doesn't agree with detaching the researcher's viewpoint from the research, the research subjects, and the effects of the research."

"He's actually telling me that, as an evaluator, I must examine the wider effects of my evaluation, that I can't say 'I've done a good evaluation using validated and reliable tools, and all the rest is the intervention people's responsibility.'"

"Exactly," I nodded.

"A man after my own heart. What else does he say?"

"He speaks about what he thinks is the unbreakable connection between reality and practice, and theory; between human life experience and objective reality. And in that context he cites Dewey (1938), who discusses the ostensible dualism of practice on the one hand and theory on the other."

"But if everything is context-dependent, culture-dependent, and dependent on the local perception of a life worth living, don't we have a problem of relativism? What if the evaluated community thinks that the intervention program money should come to them instead of funding all sorts of programs?"

"First, let's try to understand what Alexander means by 'a life that is worth living. Alexander cites Charles Taylor's (Smith, 2002) claim that day-to-day human endeavor is always subject to supreme values, which he calls 'strong values,' such as the sanctity of life, loyalty, and friendship—values that indicate for us a life worth living and the nature of a just society in the transcendental sense. It is this transcendental nature that we must research, not the immediate demands or dogmatic concepts of members of society."

"How do you translate this transcendentalism into action?"

"Alexander doesn't expand on that, but I think that you simply speak to it in its own language."

"Speak to it?"

"I'll give you an example. A researcher examined the use of purified wastewater in the Palestinian Authority (Nasrallah, 2013). Because of the Muslim laws of ritual purity and also the stigma attached to wastewater, the residents preferred using contaminated water, not purified wastewater. This necessitated long negotiations with the community's religious leaders, but with much goodwill from both sides. Ideological and religious considerations were discussed, and a compromise was reached: the purified water would be used to irrigate trees, which have a purification system of their own, but not to irrigate vegetables. Although this isn't about evaluation or research, the notion of going along with the community's transcendental values and not against them, speaking their language and not using rational reasoning or coercion, seems to me to be well suited to the intention. And most important, this enabled the use of purified wastewater for the benefit of the community without impairing its ideological coherence."

"Meaning—if I'm managing to follow what Alexander proposes—I must conduct an in-depth study to expose the community's underlying ideological and normative constructs and go with them? Not my values or those of the intervention people, because they're irrelevant."

"Yes. To go back to Ulrich, the values that your evaluation should promote are the underlying ideological constructs of the community within which the intervention is conducted."

"Is that practical?"

"That's another question entirely. What Alexander proposes is a matter of principle."

"And, as with so many in-principle answers, the practical ones only move further away."

"That's true," I agreed.

"Okay, so let's try to understand the principles."

"Alexander doesn't stop at the modern pragmatists," I said. "He cites ancient authorities, going back to Aristotle (1994), who drew a distinction between two types of knowledge: *sophia,* which deals with theories on how the world works, and *phronesis,* knowledge that enables us to function reasonably and reflectively in the world, and suggests shifting the emphasis from *phronesis* to *sophia.*"

"Why *sophia?*"

"Because it attempts to understand both a physical and metaphysical reality. Even though *sophia* has reasons, it also has a purpose, and that's what I think is important. For *sophia* attempts to understand the world by means of two processes: *techne,* which attempts to reveal the reasons for things, and *episteme,* which focuses on the purpose of things, their final outcome. But more than that, *episteme* is essentially teleological since it draws things toward their proper natural state, which connects with their essence."

"And the essence is always broader than the concrete reason," he remarked.

"According to Aristotle, it certainly is," I replied. "In his view, the teleological explanation is more complete, more essential, and more fundamental since it connects things with the complete metaphysical reality—to something wider and bigger than the local reality."

"In other words, we have to strive not only toward understanding the essence of things, but to allow the essence of things to guide our research. So evaluation has to be teleological? Aimed at a transcendental purpose?"

I nodded. "As I understand it. While, in my opinion, the type of knowledge used in evaluation is *phronesis*, but what I do adopt from Alexander is our need as evaluators to examine the implications of our evaluation transcendentally, to look forward at the possible implications of our work through the evaluees' eyes and their underlying perception of a life worth living."

"And that's the compass you use? Is it really possible?"

"Not completely. We're only human and we have limitations and pressures. But as far as possible, it's important to try to take these things into account."

"So what do we do with this transcendental scale? It demands a broad canvas that's hard to contain."

"This whole discussion began because you came along with the broad picture, one that's broader than the evaluation's goals."

"Yes," he sighed, "and now I've gotten myself into a bigger tangle."

"The man who tries to resolve that tangle is again Ulrich (2005, 2012)."

"What does he suggest?"

"Ulrich both follows Churchman and takes issue with him. Among other things, Churchman is thought to be one of the fathers of the systems approach in management and social research (1968b). His most difficult question is 'How can we design improvement in a large system without understanding the whole system?'(1968a, 1968b, 1971)."

"It's impossible," my colleague said.

"So if it's impossible, how can we understand a system?"

"Good question."

"And Churchman's answer is to 'sweep in' all the information—of any kind—that can be collected regarding the system in question."

"No more and no less?"

"Ulrich took Churchman's concepts of 'sweeping in' and 'whole system judgment' a step further. He talks about 'boundary judgment' instead of judging the whole system."

"And where does he go from there?"

"What's interesting is the difference between them," I said. "Churchman aspired to an overall understanding, whereas Ulrich speaks about means of critical reasoning: 'the story I mean to tell.' He contends that since it is impossible to contain the entire system, the question of boundary judgment becomes obvious. Using his systems approach—'critical systems heuristics' (CSH)—he contends that our perception of a system, its boundaries and contents, is usually heuristic and intuitive, and that's not good enough. In order to be able to discuss a system, we first have to know what is this system. Therefore, we must critically examine its boundaries."

"So what Ulrich is telling me is in fact this: 'Know what you're talking about.'"

"Yes, that's what he says. And your decision about what's relevant, what's important, what should be included, and what can be left out should be an informed critical process, not a heuristic and intuitive one."

"So how do you make these decisions? Are there guidelines?"

"There are all kinds of guidelines in all sorts of articles, but the main thing is to go with your central aim (Ulrich, 2005). That might be the definition of a problem or of a situation, a suggestion for resolving a problem, a question, and so forth. The aim must be of good quality, where the criterion for quality is its relevance to the players. Theoretical support and precise formulation are far less important and, in and of themselves, are insufficient."

"Like all pragmatists."

"Yes. With this in mind, it's easier for you to decide what's important enough to be included in the system you're examining, and what's less important. Who must be in it and what can be left out. This process enables you to focus without needing to include the whole of France in your deliberations."

"You can laugh," he said, as I smiled. "I accept it with love."

"I'm not laughing; I'm part of your deliberations."

"Let's assume that in my case, the part of the community that's less mobile is important for me because it's less educated and is employed in work with no possibility of advancement."

"And the traditional leadership, the educated young people, and the connection between them. The reciprocal effects," I added. "It's hard to do it all in one go. Every such group has considerations for and against."

"At least there's one thing about which I'm no longer deliberating," my colleague said with some relief.

"And that is?" I asked.

"The unholy alliance. From everything we've talked about, it's completely clear that as an evaluator, and certainly as an expert evaluator, I don't have the option of remaining within the limits of the program and examining it from the goals inward."

"No, you don't, at least not according to the philosophers whose opinions we've discussed."

"Oh yeah," my colleague said. "The inevitable conclusion of this entire conversation is that evaluators must take into account where their evaluation is leading. We have to address its implications and the effects it might have in the broadest possible sense, far beyond the question of the nature and quality of the program or its expansion or termination."

NEW DIRECTIONS FOR EVALUATION • DOI: 10.1002/ev

"And we've also learned something no less important," I added, "that the most significant criterion for examining the implications and effects of an evaluation isn't our personal worldview, nor that of the intervention people; rather, the significant criterion is in the effects on and worldview of those who'll be affected by those implications and effects: the evaluees and their environment."

My colleague concluded. "As evaluators, we bear a very great social responsibility: to look broadly, to look forward, to be responsible for our actions, and as far as possible, to be sure that the purpose is indeed for the benefit of those who will ultimately be affected by our work."

I nodded silently.

References

Alexander, H. A. (2006). A view from somewhere: Explaining the paradigms of educational research. *Journal of Philosophy of Education, 40*(2), 205–217.

Arav, N. (2010). Man solely as a means? Evaluation in light of the Kantian imperative. In M. Levin-Rozalis & R. Savaya (Eds.), *Evaluation in Israel: Issues and dilemmas* (pp. 333–342). Beer Sheva, Israel: Ben-Gurion University of the Negev. (in Hebrew)

Aristotle. (1994). *Metaphysics* (D. Bostoc, Trans.). Oxford, England: Clarendon Press.

Churchman, C. W. (1968a). *Challenge to reason.* New York, NY: McGraw-Hill.

Churchman, C. W. (1968b). *The systems approach.* New York, NY: Delacorte Press.

Churchman, C. W. (1971). *The design of inquiring systems,* New York, NY: Basic Books.

Cousins, J. B., & Whitmore, E. (1998). Framing participatory evaluation. In E. Whitmore (Ed.), *Understanding and practicing participatory evaluation. New Directions for Evaluation, 80,* 5–24.

Dewey, J. (1938). *Logic: A theory of inquiry,* New York, NY: Henry Holt.

Fetterman, D. M. (1994). Empowerment evaluation. *Evaluation Practice, 15*(1), 1–15.

Friedman, J. V., Rothman, J., & Withers, B. (2006). The power of why: Engaging the goal paradox in program evaluation. *American Journal of Evaluation, 27*(2), 201–218.

Greene, J. C. (2000). Challenges in practicing deliberative democratic evaluation. In K. E. Ryan (Ed.), *Evaluation as a democratic process: promoting inclusion, dialogue, and deliberation. New Directions for Evaluation, 85,* 13–26.

Guba, E. G., & Lincoln, Y. S. (1989). *Fourth generation evaluation.* London, England: Sage.

Kant, I. (1991). *The metaphysics of morals* (Mary Gregor, Trans.). Cambridge, England: Cambridge University Press.

Levin-Rozalis, M. (2010). Cybernetics: A possible solution for the "knowledge gap" between "internal" and "external" in an evaluation process. *Evaluation and Program Planning, 33*(4), 333–342.

Nasrallah, W. M. (2013). *Wastewater and solid waste projects in the West Bank— Success versus failure* (Unpublished master's thesis). Ben-Gurion University of the Negev.

Smith, N. H. (2002). *Charles Taylor: Meaning, morals, and modernity.* Cambridge, England: Polity.

Ulrich, W. (2001). The quest for competence in systemic research and practice. *Systems Research and Behavioral Science, 18*(1), 3–28.

Ulrich, W. (2005). *A brief introduction to critical systems heuristics (CSH)*. Milton Keynes, England: The Open University. Retrieved from http://wulrich.com/downloads /ulrich_2005f.pdf

Ulrich, W. (2012). CST's two ways: A concise account of critical systems thinking. *Ulrich's Bimonthly*. Retrieved from http://wulrich.com/downloads/bimonthly_ november2012.pdf

MIRI LEVIN-ROZALIS, *a founding and current member of IAPE (the Israeli Association for Program Evaluation), has conducted, taught, researched, and written about evaluation for more than 30 years as a senior faculty member at Ben-Gurion University of the Negev, the Weizmann Institute of Science, and independently.*

Lapidot-Lefler, N., Friedman, V. J., Arieli, D., Haj, N., Sykes, I., & Kais, N. (2015). Social space and field as constructs for evaluating social inclusion. In B. Rosenstein & H. Desivilya Syna (Eds.), *Evaluation and social justice in complex sociopolitical contexts. New Directions for Evaluation, 146*, 33–43.

3

Social Space and Field as Constructs for Evaluating Social Inclusion

Noam Lapidot-Lefler, Victor J. Friedman, Daniella Arieli, Noha Haj, Israel Sykes, Nasreen Kais

Abstract

This paper addresses the role of evaluation in promoting social inclusion, an important component of social justice, with a focus on exclusion resulting from physical disability. We argue that the evaluation of social exclusion and social inclusion requires evaluators not only to reconsider their role and methods, but also to revise the fundamental constructs through which they study how programs and other interventions generate change at the individual, group, community, and societal levels. Drawing on field theory, we suggest that social inclusion processes can be understood and assessed in terms of the expansion of individuals' life space, which consists of social, political, cultural, and resource dimensions. The paper illustrates these constructs with data from a participative action evaluation of a pilot program for providing services to people with disabilities in Israel. Our aim in developing these constructs is to provide not only tools for assessment, but also ways of thinking that may enable socially excluded people to be more active agents of inclusion. © 2015 Wiley Periodicals, Inc., and the American Evaluation Association.

S ocial exclusion and social inclusion have increasingly been used to address the idea of social justice as ensuring access for and protection of disadvantaged groups (Riddell, 2009). Social exclusion can be defined as a multidimensional, dynamic socioeconomic process that deprives particular individuals and groups of participation in the key activities and benefits of the society in which they live (Hills, Le Grand, & Pichaud, 2002). These groups are usually associated with economic (for example, poverty), racial, ethnic, religious, physical (for example, disability), or other differences that mark them off from the mainstream.

The Social Exclusion Knowledge Network (SEKN) of the World Health Organization (WHO) Commission on Social Determinants of Health (Popay et al., 2008) argued for a *relational* (versus *static*) understanding of social exclusion as a process that deprives people of participation as full and valued members of society. Social exclusion is driven by unequal power relationships interacting across economic, political, social, and cultural dimensions and at the individual, household, group, community, country, and global levels. These processes generate a continuum of inclusion/exclusion characterized by unequal access to resources, capabilities, and rights. In other words, exclusion cannot be understood simply in terms of access to material and social benefits, but also in terms of the social relationships in which those benefits are embedded.

Evaluating Social Exclusion/Inclusion as a "Field" Phenomenon

Mertens (2008) applied the social justice theory of ethics to the relationship between evaluation and social inclusion. She argued that the ethical responsibility of evaluators goes beyond avoiding harm and treating every person with respect. Rather, evaluators' ethical responsibility means giving precedence, or at least equal weight, to the voices of groups who may not have sufficient power for accurate representation and enabling excluded populations to take an active role as agents in social change (Mertens, 2008). We agree with Mertens, but argue that the relational nature of social exclusion/inclusion requires the development of innovative methods for assessing as well as for fostering inclusion. We propose that *social space* and *field theory* provide constructs for capturing relational processes of social exclusion/inclusion with a high level of fidelity. Furthermore, we suggest these constructs can help excluded populations act as more effective agents of their own inclusion.

Social space and field theory were central to the work of the social psychologist Kurt Lewin (1936) and the sociologist Pierre Bourdieu (1993; Bourdieu & Wacquant, 1992). Both men built their innovative social science on the philosophy of Ernst Cassirer (see Friedman, 2011), who made a distinction between a *substantialist* and a *relational* logic of reality (Cassirer, 1961). *Substantialism* holds that reality is composed of concrete, independent *things* that can be observed through our senses. *Relationalism*, on the other hand, holds that reality is best grasped as an *ordering* of elements of perception through a mental *process* of construction that gives them intelligibility and meaning.

According to this approach, space is not a physical concept, but rather a mental creation that can be used to *think relationally* about making order from any given set of elements. Lewin and Bourdieu adopted this idea of space as an essential construct for theorizing about the social world.

They borrowed the concept of *field* from physics as a way of accounting for causality in social space. Spaces are fields because they exert force on and shape the behavior of the people and groups that comprise them. Fields are both phenomenal and structural, linking the internal world of people with the external social world through an ongoing shaping process. Fields can be conceptualized as configurations of social space characterized by four dimensions: (a) the individual and collective *actors* who constitute the field; (b) the relationships among these actors, with a particular focus on relative power; (c) the shared meanings that make the field intelligible and hold it together; and (d) the "rules of the game" that govern action within it (Fligstein & McAdam, 2011; Friedman, 2011).

Processes of social exclusion/inclusion occur when (a) fields are comprised of groups that are marked by difference, (b) the relationships among these groups are characterized by inequality, (c) the meanings attributed to difference are characterized by stigma, and (d) the rules of the game prevent particular groups from fully participating in society. As a field phenomenon, social exclusion/inclusion is generated by social norms that shape the behavior of people and as cognitive structures that become internalized and influence how people perceive themselves and the world around them. Every time people act according to these cognitive structures, they reinforce the field and the behaviors and attitudes it shapes.

Viewing social exclusion/inclusion as field phenomena implies that programs aimed at inclusion ought to lead to observable changes in the field over time. Furthermore, observing field changes means assessing changes in the way excluded individuals perceive their worlds and the social norms that shape these perceptions. Lewin's concept of *life space* provides a very useful conceptual tool for assessing these processes. The life space is composed of all the perceived elements that determine the behavior of an individual at any given moment. It reflects the total range of behaviors that are possible and not possible for that person in a given situation (Lewin, 1936). Each change in a person's life space means either expanding or contracting the *space of free movement* (Lewin, 1936), which Lewin defined as the range of what is possible for a person at any given moment.

We argue that processes of social exclusion/inclusion can be observed by mapping changes in the life space of individuals. This kind of mapping can provide evaluators with a tool for assessing the degree to which programs generate social inclusion among their recipients. We came to this insight through reflection on a participative stakeholder evaluation that we carried out with an innovative program for people with disabilities. In the following sections, we describe the program, the evaluation, and how the evaluation findings can be used to conceptualize social inclusion as change in the life space.

Evaluating a Program for an Excluded Population

Pathways to the Community was established and funded by Israel Unlimited, a strategic partnership between Joint Distribution Committee (JDC)–Israel, the government of Israel, and the Ruderman Family Foundation, for development of services to promote independent living and integration of adults with disabilities into the community. The program is aimed at developing an innovative approach to providing services in small cities and rural areas to people with disabilities, ages 21–65, who have not utilized rehabilitation and/or employment services. The Action Research Center for Social Justice at the Yezreel Valley College conducted a formative *action evaluation* (Rothman, 2012) of the program during its two-year pilot stage in order to generate a model that could be adopted and disseminated by the Ministry of Welfare.

The pilot took place in a small city whose inhabitants are Arab-Palestinian citizens of Israel. The partners included the municipal government, the Ministry of Welfare, JDC-Israel, and a local nongovernmental organization (NGO) that administered the program and offered its Senior Citizen Center as a meeting facility. The first stage of the evaluation was to involve all the stakeholders in setting program goals and developing a logic model. This stage began with two workshops introducing participatory practice to potential candidates who had never been involved in such processes. In the course of the workshops, it became clear that the families of the candidates comprised a separate stakeholder group, and a series of workshops was held especially with them.

After the workshops, members of all the stakeholder groups (N=34)[1] responded to a written, open questionnaire asking (a) what their definitions of success (goals) were for the proposed program, (b) *why* these goals were important to them personally, (c) how these goals could be achieved in practice, and (d) what their dreams were for this program. These questionnaires were analyzed separately for each stakeholder group to first identify program goals as perceived by each group. The 34 respondents then met in two separate groups, each of which included members of all the stakeholder groups, to talk together about why this program was important to them (Friedman, Rothman, & Withers, 2006). Next, each stakeholder group met separately to agree on its goals for the program. Representatives of all the stakeholder groups then met to define common program goals, develop a unified program logic model, and plan action. The planning stage culminated with a one-day conference held at the college, during which the logic model was presented to its sponsors, and members of all the stakeholder groups reflected on the participative process.

The program began with 12 "members," with the goal of reaching 25 within two years. It involved twice-weekly meetings at the Senior Citizen Center as well as services received at home and in the community according to an individual plan developed together with the Program Coordinator. An "Operations Committee" representing all the stakeholder groups monitored the program's implementation, providing support and advice to the Coordinator.

A first round of formative evaluation was carried out in August 2013. The evaluation focused on (a) qualitatively assessing progress toward achievement of program goals, (b) changes that had occurred, or not occurred, in the lives of each member since joining the program, (c) the program dimensions that contributed to these changes, (d) the participative process and its effects, and (e) recruitment of new members. The evaluation team conducted in-depth interviews with 26 stakeholders (9 program participants, 6 family members, 5 professionals/sponsors, and 6 student volunteers). The interview data were analyzed and presented separately to three main stakeholder groups: the participants, the families, and the professionals/sponsors. The separate meetings enabled stakeholders to review the evaluators' analysis of *their* data before it was seen by other stakeholders and reports were written.

Assessing Social Inclusion as an Expansion of the Life Space

Evaluation findings pointed to significant positive changes in the lives of most of the program members. However, it is not the goal of this paper to evaluate the program's effectiveness or to evaluate the theory of change implicit in the logic model. Rather, our goal is to use these findings (1) to illustrate how processes of social inclusion can be conceptualized as an expansion of the life space and (2) to suggest how evaluators might use this construct as an evaluation tool.

To integrate concepts of life space and exclusion, we have merged our conceptualization of field as actors, relationships, meanings, and rules of the game (Friedman, 2011) with the SEKH Model of social exclusion as comprised of social, political, cultural, and economic dimensions (Popay et al., 2008). In doing so, we have merged the actors and relationships components into a single, social dimension. We have also added the economic dimension, which we have reframed as the *resource* dimension so as to account for both material and nonmaterial resources.

The *social* dimension of the life space refers to a sense of belonging based on the extent, nature, and strength of an individual's relationships (Friedman, 2011). Prior to the program, the social dimension was characterized by a very narrow circle of people with whom they had contact— mostly their families—and a set of relationships heavily determined by hierarchy and dependence. This change was reflected in the wide range of new relationships that the members established, especially in meeting other people with disabilities:

> *Member:* Everyone here has problems like me.... It's very useful hearing others talk about their difficulties and problems. It helps learning from each other. The members of the group...give me hope and I like when they talk....It makes me happy.

The sense of belonging was reflected in the fact that they described themselves as "members," the program as a "family," and their relationships like that of "brothers and sisters." Through the program, members also created new, more egalitarian relationships with service providers, researchers, and students—all of which contributed to an expansion of the life space.

The participatory evaluation process, which emphasized partnership, played a role in decreasing the hierarchical relationship between members, their families, and the service providers:

> *A family member:* Of course I feel like a partner.... We families really need this space for expressing ourselves.... What was really meaningful was that there is a person with disabilities who feels like he is not worth anything and suddenly you give him a real place and that he is really able. It's a wonderful feeling.

The process also put them into relationships of partnership with people from completely new walks of life, such as academic researchers and students.

The most significant finding was that participation in the program was associated with an expansion of the social dimension beyond the program itself:

> *Member:* (The program) was new for me and a little bit difficult, but I was able to overcome (the difficulties).... I began to visit friends.... I got over the isolation. I was always sitting home alone and wouldn't leave home. I wouldn't visit friends because I was in a wheelchair and there was no accessibility. But today I visit my friends despite the wheelchair and lack of accessibility.

This quotation reflects not only the expansion of the person's social circle but also the psychological nature of the change. While the physical conditions themselves did not change, they no longer kept the person at home and in isolation.

The *resource* dimension refers to access to material and nonmaterial resources such as money, services, knowledge, and social capital. Prior to the program, resources were theoretically available to people with disabilities in the community, but they were not utilized due to lack of awareness, accessibility, or motivation. Even if the community was offering these resources, they were nonexistent in the life space of these people. The program created a space that was rich in information, knowledge, skill development, and other resources. The members talked about how they benefited from specific courses or activities. By raising awareness, defining needs, and making resources more accessible, the program played an important role in expanding the life space of the members. Furthermore, the individual plan functioned as a tool through which members could reflect on and expand their life space.

The *cultural* dimension refers to the dominant meanings—values, norms, and attitudes—that a particular society attributes to difference and diversity. In this case, the strong negative stigma about disability had instilled powerful feelings of shame:

> *Member:* My world expanded....After I became ill, I was either at home or in the hospital. I didn't go out and didn't do anything. Today I go out to the coffee shop, shopping, and to do other things that I hadn't dared to do beforehand.... Today I have a lot more courage.

It was not the lack of physical accessibility that kept the person at home, but rather the fear of being seen with a disability. The courage came from the fact that this person no longer saw his disability as a source of shame. Participation in the program led members to see themselves beyond their disability:

> *Member:* I am happy. I found interesting things and feel as if I have found myself here.... I feel as if I am important, that I help others, that I am worthwhile...I have gotten to something.

> *Member:* I feel as if I have returned to myself. I work and I have started to learn English here. I return home feeling that I do something, important things. I tell my wife what I do here.

The life spaces of these people expanded to open up regions of their selves that were either new or had been inaccessible to them. Rather than feeling shame about their disability, they now see themselves as "important" and "worthwhile."

Finally, the *political* dimension refers to the "rules of the game" governing power and the distribution of opportunity to participate in public life, to express desires, and to have interests taken into account. Given the stigma attached to disability, the rules of the game in this particular community were that people with disability should stay out of the public eye. However, change in the political dimension was evident in interactions between members and their families:

> *Member:* At home, they say I have become difficult.... I am always talking and saying what I want.

Family member: Before the program, she had requests but always with tears in her eyes. Now it's different.... She asks for things but with a good feeling and she is more satisfied.

Family member: Now she feels important. She feels that she can express her opinion, speak and tell.... I feel she is stronger, changed.

As these quotes indicate, prior to the program the tacit rules of their life space led the people with disabilities to avoid asking for help because they questioned the legitimacy of their needs. Furthermore, they felt they had to keep their opinions to themselves. Afterwards, they increasingly began to express and advocate for what they wanted. They felt they had things to say and more freely voiced their opinions. This expansion of the life space was experienced as a change in the person's "world" and that of their families.

Another significant political change concerned accessibility. One of the members explained that, prior to the program, if she were invited to events and tried to attend, but faced an inaccessible barrier along the way (for example, stairs), she would simply return home feeling ashamed. However, after participating in the program, she changed her behavior and waited there until the hosts found a way of enabling her to attend. In her words, "they should feel ashamed, not me!"

The larger field in which these people lived, internalized in their life space, literally kept them "in their place" of exclusion (Friedman & Sykes, 2012). In all of these examples from the political dimension, the change was first psychological, in the sense that a social norm was no longer internalized and accepted by the person. In rejecting these exclusionary norms, they expanded their life space and new possibilities opened up for them. In doing so, they acted as agents of their own inclusion. Furthermore, these changes in the life space had the potential for changing the larger field since others had to respond to these demands for legitimacy and inclusion.

These dimensions can be assessed and mapped onto a visual representation of the life space. Each dimension represents a continuum. For

Figure 3.1. Mapping the Life Space

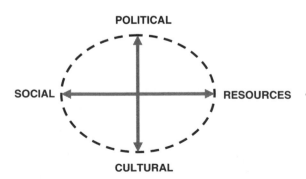

Figure 3.2. Mapping Inclusion as Change in the Life Space

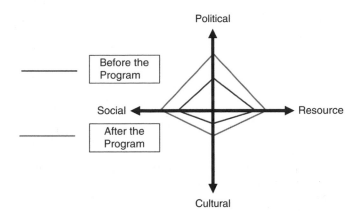

example, the social dimension would extend from few highly unequal relationships and a weak sense of belonging to a large number of equal relationships with a strong sense of belonging. The resource dimension would extend from few resources to a large number and variety of resources. The cultural dimension would extend from a high degree of internalized stigma to a lack of internalized stigma. The political dimension would extend from many and powerful rules of the game that limit participation to rules that promote inclusion.

Specific indicators could be developed for each dimension in which scales could be created to make them roughly measurable. While having little significance in absolute terms, quantification would enable people with disabilities to track changes in their life space over time (see Figure 3.2). It would facilitate the development of instruments for evaluating the effectiveness of programs in promoting social inclusion among a particular group of people. Furthermore, such instruments could be used to help people with disabilities, as well as other excluded populations, become more conscious of their life space and how to expand it. Clearly, an instrument for assessing the life space of individuals would be incomplete without complementary instruments for assessing and challenging the structural relationships that generate exclusion. Nevertheless, a self-assessment instrument for reflection, learning, and action planning would enhance the ability of excluded people to become more effective agents of their own inclusion.

Note

1. People with disabilities (12), family members (10), JDC-Israel (2), Ministry of Welfare (3), Municipal Welfare Bureau (2), Senior Citizens NGO (4).

References

Bourdieu, P. (1993). *The field of cultural production.* Cambridge, England: Polity Press.

Bourdieu, P., & Wacquant, L. (1992). *An introduction to reflexive sociology.* Cambridge, England: Polity Press.

Cassirer, E. (1961). *The logic of the humanities.* New Haven, CT: Yale University Press.

Fligstein, N., & McAdam, D. (2011). Toward a general theory of strategic action fields. *Sociological Theory, 29*, 1–26.

Friedman, V. J. (2011). Revisiting social space: relational thinking about organizational change. In A. B. (Rami) Shani, R. W. Woodman, & W.A. Pasmore (Eds.), *Research in Organizational Change and Development, 19*, 233–257.

Friedman, V., Rothman, J., & Withers, B. (2006). The power of why: Engaging the goal paradox in program evaluation. *American Journal of Evaluation, 27*(2), 1–18.

Friedman, V., & Sykes, I. (2012). Can the concept "social space" reveal a deep structure for the theory and practice of organizational learning? In A. Berthoin Antal, P. Meusberger, & L. Saursana (Eds.), *Learning organizations: Extending the field.* Dordrecht, Germany: Springer Science and Business Media.

Hills, J., Le Grand, J., & Piachaud, D. (2002). *Understanding social exclusion.* Oxford, England: Oxford University Press.

Lewin, K. (1936). *Principles of topological psychology.* New York, NY: McGraw-Hill.

Mertens, D. (2008). Transformative considerations: Inclusion and social justice. *American Journal of Evaluation, 28*(1), 86–90.

Popay, J., Escorel, S., Hernández, M., Johnston, H., Mathieson, J., & Rispel, L. (2008). *Understanding and tackling social exclusion: Final report to the WHO commission on social determinants of health from the Social Exclusion Knowledge Network.* Retrieved from http://www.who.int/social_determinants/knowledge_networks/final_reports/sekn_fin al%20report_042008.pdf

Riddell, S. (2009). Social justice, equality and inclusion in Scottish education, *Discourse, 30*(3), 283–297.

Rothman, J. (2012). Action evaluation in theory and practice. In J. Rothman (Ed.), *From identity-based conflict to identity-based cooperation* (pp. 125–134). New York, NY: Springer.

NOAM LAPIDOT-LEFLER *is a lecturer at the Department of Behavioral Sciences and Education, The Max Stern Yezreel Valley College, and at the Department of Special Education, The Faculty of Education, Oranim College for Education, Israel, whose main research topic centers on the field of education, focusing on special education social spaces.*

VICTOR J. FRIEDMAN *is an associate professor of organizational behavior and the director of the Action Research Center for Social Justice at the Max Stern Yezreel Valley College, Israel.*

DANIELLA ARIELI *is a social anthropologist, a lecturer, and a member of the Action Research Center for Social Justice at the Max Stern Yezreel Valley College, Israel.*

NOHA HAJ *is a researcher at the Action Research Center for Social Justice at the Max Stern Yezreel Valley College and a student in the master's program in the management of informal educational systems at Bar Ilan University, Israel.*

ISRAEL SYKES *lives in Jerusalem, where he works as a freelance organizational consultant, action researcher, and translator.*

NESREEN KAIS *is a research assistant at the Action Research Center for Social Justice at the Max Stern Yezreel Valley College and a master's student in psychology at Tel Aviv University.*

NEW DIRECTIONS FOR EVALUATION • DOI: 10.1002/ev

Desivilya Syna, H., Rottman, A., & Raz, M. (2015). Social justice in action: The contribution of evaluation to employment integration of a vulnerable population—The case of college graduates with learning disabilities. In B. Rosenstein & H. Desivilya Syna (Eds.), *Evaluation and social justice in complex sociopolitical contexts. New Directions for Evaluation, 146*, 45–55.

4

Social Justice in Action: The Contribution of Evaluation to Employment Integration of a Vulnerable Population—The Case of College Graduates With Learning Disabilities

Helena Desivilya Syna, Amit Rottman, Michal Raz

Abstract

This article presents and discusses an evaluation model that can contribute to social justice and that increases equal opportunities of employment for a vulnerable population—college graduates with learning disabilities. The framework responds to increasingly competitive job markets' potential exclusion of vulnerable social groups from meaningful participation in this domain, consequently impeding social justice. Counteracting socioeconomic gaps in societies requires active involvement of community members, social institutions, and government. According to the proposed model, the evaluator assumes such an active stance by building genuine partnership with evaluees. We present the sociopolitical and socioeconomic context—the "brave" new job market foreshadowing the evaluation and social justice interface. The model is illustrated through a case study—evaluation of an innovative program supporting the transition of learning disabled college graduates to the job market. © 2015 Wiley Periodicals, Inc., and the American Evaluation Association.

T his article presents an evaluation model that can contribute to fostering social justice by promoting equal opportunities in employment integration of a vulnerable population—college graduates with learning disabilities. We open with portraying the sociopolitical realities of the current job market, which foreshadows the evaluation–social justice interface. Subsequently, the evaluation model is presented, followed by a description of the evaluated project, highlighting the implementation modes of the model. Finally, we reflect upon the insights regarding the role of the proposed evaluation model in fostering social justice.

The Characteristics of the "Brave" New Job Market

Economic and political transformations have markedly affected job markets in the developed world. These changes are visibly manifested in the odds and nature of employment; namely, participation in the job market at any given time (Stuart, Grugulis, Tomlinson, Forde, & MacKenzie, 2013).

Most of the developed countries have been facing economic recession, including employment crises. In response to these economic predicaments, governments have applied austerity measures inspired by neoliberal ideology. Consequently, labor markets have become increasingly competitive, leading to mounting inequalities among various social strata. The political networks and lobbies have promoted opportunities for the dominant groups while leaving the other members of the society lingering behind (Bidwell, Briscoe, Fernandez-Mateo, & Sterling, 2013). These economic and sociopolitical trends have affected social groups with special needs most profoundly. In lieu of support, the vulnerable individuals stand the highest risk of exclusion from meaningful participation in the job market.

Stuart and colleagues (2013) emphasized the flimsy nature of previously achieved social safeguards in light of international competition and the politics of flexible labor markets. Fading protection measures have precipitated mounting social inequalities. To counteract the adverse effects of a political economy of insecurity reflected in growing socioeconomic gaps, the active involvement of communities, social institutions, and government is necessary (Beck, 2000). In line with this contention, and drawing on Polanyi, Stuart and colleagues (2013) argue for a revival of the social justice agenda in order to affirm moral economy; namely, a countermovement designed to change the nature and dynamics of labor markets.

Scholars have expressed their concern with regard to equal opportunities of college graduates' employability. In the current era of uncertainty, graduates of academic institutions need to adopt a proactive orientation, to self-manage and maneuver in the job market while developing their careers. Moreau and Leathwood (2006) challenge the neoliberal assumption of meritocracy, arguing that factors such as social class, gender, ethnicity, age, disability, and university attendance significantly affect the graduates' employability prospects. The emphasis placed on individual responsibility, while overlooking social inequalities, bears potentially negative implications for vulnerable college graduates. Thus, individuals with special needs may find it particularly difficult to embrace a proactive stance in marketing their merits, which in turn reduces their chances of inclusion in the labor market (Bridgstock, 2009).

The Interface of Social Justice and Evaluation

The concern for social groups with special needs, while attempting to promote their human rights and equal opportunities, constitutes a central component of social justice. An active role of the evaluators in this regard enables the program participants to express their voices, thereby implanting the social issue on the public agenda (Lincoln, 1993).

The current article focuses on the role of evaluation in enhancing social justice for a vulnerable social group, the participants of the evaluated program, but also to some extent by the program initiators and the program staff. Drawing on Rawls's (1999) conceptualization of social justice, we examine the potential contribution of evaluation to coping with inequalities and power imbalances in society, thereby fostering equal access to opportunities in the job market. According to Rawls, social justice means guaranteeing and protecting equal access to civil freedoms, human rights, and opportunities, and defending the most disadvantaged members of society.

An active stance of evaluators in promoting social justice is reflected in studying the social issue, investigating the implementation of a program designed to engage the core of this social concern. Since research rests on systematic data collection, its products may provide evidence-based information and thereby amplify the stakeholders' voices. The quality of usable knowledge improves due to the participation of various stakeholders in the research process, provided that cooperative relations among the stakeholders and evaluators have indeed been established. Such bonds enhance the odds of pooling together resources and sharing knowledge, thus promoting social goals (Desivilya Syna & Palgi, 2011).

The Evaluation Model: Enhancing Social Justice for Vulnerable Social Groups—Social Justice in Action

The proposed model addresses the complexity of the evaluator–evaluee relationships while underscoring the strengths and challenges of collaborative bonds and their potential contribution to social justice.

This framework draws on Abma and Widdershoven's (2008) typology concerning evaluator–evaluee relations, emphasizing the potential impact of social and organizational elements, such as power and other contextual features, on program quality and success. The classification distinguishes four kinds of evaluator bonds with the stakeholders, each corresponding to different traditions of evaluation.

1. *Uninvolved Relationships* (the objectivist traditions of evaluation; Scriven, 1997) stem from the underlying assumption that social relations are irrelevant to evaluation research. Hence, the evaluator embraces the professional stance of an objective and impartial researcher by refraining from engagement in any social processes or issues to be advanced by the evaluated project. According to this approach, forging relationships with evaluees, especially involvement in political dynamics, is considered a source of bias and potential contamination of the research results.

2. *Instrumental Relationships* (utilization-oriented evaluation; Patton, 1997) are based on the premise that social relations should be managed in order to promote learning. Consequently, the evaluator functions mainly as a consultant, attempting to develop relationships with the evaluees in a way that fosters utilization of the evaluation findings, thus maximizing learning processes and in turn improving the project's quality.

3. The *Changing Relationships* approach (empowerment, democratic, participatory, feminist evaluation; Fetterman, 1994; Greene, 2001; Mertens, 2002) builds on recognition of the political dimension in evaluation and the need to promote transformation from asymmetrical social relations between the dominant groups and the vulnerable groups into socially just bonds. Hence, the evaluator's role is to promote social change through democratic, cooperative processes and active participation of all the partners and stakeholders.

4. *Building Relationships as the Essence of Evaluation* (relational and care traditions; Guba & Lincoln, 1981; Parlett & Hamilton, 1972; Stake, 1991) constitutes the fundamental element of the role of the evaluation and the evaluator. Maintaining dialogue among the parties (including the evaluator) on an equal basis constitutes the major aim in this evaluation approach. The evaluator functions primarily as a facilitator and guide while emphasizing horizontal, nonhierarchical approaches and friendly relationships.

To promote social justice—specifically, to increase the odds of equal employment opportunities for a vulnerable social group—our model emphasizes an active stance of the evaluator in placing the social issue on the public agenda (Stuart et al., 2013). Such orientation enhances the voices and empowers the vulnerable group and agents of change acting on their behalf. The model integrates the changing relations approach in Abma and Widdershoven's typology with the notion of a genuine partnership. The central dimensions of a partnership revolve around non-hierarchical mutual relationships, built on a cooperative exchange of resources, joint responsibility and decision-making geared to attaining shared goals. Scholars have made a distinction between genuine partnership based on mutual trust among the parties and a pragmatic form aimed at distribution of risks, mainly following self-interest (Desivilya Syna & Palgi, 2011).

Developing genuine partnerships means building relationships among the partners through four components: (1) negotiation, (2) coordination, (3) power balancing (empowerment), and (4) reflection and learning. This entails devoting parallel attention to structural and process elements. Addressing structural elements involves managing the interdependence and power relations between the partners by means of appropriate division of tasks and empowerment. The process aspects entail negotiation of purpose, developing shared vision, design and practices with regard to the partnership, constructing mechanisms for coordination of communications, knowledge sharing, decision making, and conflict engagement. Attending to both the structural and process aspects is essential for developing commitment to the partnership, building trust among partners, and integrating the embraced cooperative values with coherent action (Desivilya Syna, Rottman, & Raz, 2014).

Our model is premised on the idea that building genuine partnership between the evaluators and all the stakeholders can enhance the generation of usable and evidence based knowledge derived from a variety of perspectives (Desivilya Syna & Palgi, 2011). This in turn precipitates deeper understanding of the social issue that the program addresses, in particular comprehending the concerns of the participants, members of vulnerable and marginalized groups. Genuine partnership also corresponds to the changing relationship evaluation approach. By creating collaborative and inclusive bonds, it promotes democratic processes of mutual responsibility, involvement, and meaningful participation of all the parties through ongoing dialogue among the evaluators and the stakeholders. Genuine partnership also fosters empowerment of the program participants by recognizing the impact of the sociopolitical and socioeconomic context, consequently developing power asymmetry sensitivity (Desivilya Syna & Rottman, 2012).

Implementation of the Social Justice in Action Evaluation Model

Prior to discussing the modes of the model implementation, we present the case study.

It constitutes a follow-up investigation of an innovative program that was established to promote the employment integration of learning disabled college graduates.

A literature review and expert opinions suggested that the transition from academic studies to work–life poses marked challenges for the learning disabled (Doren, Lindstrom, Zane, & Johnson, 2007). Beyond issues related to formal learning, graduates with learning disabilities experience difficulties in the personal, interpersonal, and societal arenas.

NEW DIRECTIONS FOR EVALUATION • DOI: 10.1002/ev

The transition from academic studies to employment requires active coping in the context of increasingly competitive job market (Beck, 2000; Stuart et al., 2013): job search, getting a job, adjustment to the workplace, sustainability at work, and the development of a meaningful career. Due to the personal vulnerability of the learning disabled graduates and the harsh external circumstances, their odds of effective assimilation in the job market appear markedly mitigated. Counteracting these impediments requires a tailored-made support program. Such a project ought to offer assistance at the individual and system level (Madaus, 2008).

The support center for students with learning disabilities at a college in Northern Israel responded to this call by founding an innovative program of occupational counseling for graduates with learning disabilities. The project supports and prepares the participants for the transition into the job market. It comprises three phases: (1) an academic course and experiential workshop on the transition from college to job market, psychological and occupational evaluation, design of an individual career plan, and assistance in the job search; (2) assimilation of the graduates in workplaces, followed-up by the program staff; (3) a follow-up of program participants in their respective jobs, providing tailor-made assistance.

The program plan stipulates that the staff collaborate and coordinate its activities with occupational assistance centers, manpower organizations, governmental authorities, and employers. The project operated in an experimental mode for three years, involving more than 80 participants.

The evaluation research accompanied the program for three years, aiming to provide usable knowledge to the initiators and program staff, thereby maximizing its fit to the participants' needs. To enhance social justice for the participants—namely, to increase equal opportunities of employment—we adopted the social justice in action model: integrating the changing relations approach with building a genuine partnership.

The model was embedded in three parallel ways: (1) designing a framework which corresponded to the emerging needs in the research setting; (2) employing the formative evaluation function of changing and improving the project in the course of its operation; (3) timely transmission of the research findings to policy and decision-making bodies. Thus, the evaluation team endeavored jointly with the evaluees to grasp the theory-in-action underlying the program and look for ways to advance the project. In line with the social justice in action model, we invested considerable efforts in building a genuine partnership: developing collaborative bonds with the program initiators, the program staff, and the participants.

To learn about the project from a variety of perspectives, semistructured and open individual interviews and focus groups were conducted with the program initiators, with the staff, and with some of the students and graduates. In accordance with the model, the individual and group interviews attempted to foster dialogue among the parties while creating a cooperative climate, thus enhancing the expression of genuine voices.

NEW DIRECTIONS FOR EVALUATION • DOI: 10.1002/ev

We also analyzed the questionnaire responses of the participants concerning their perceptions of various program components. Subsequently, the evaluators and the program staff jointly developed tools for documenting the participation patterns of the program participants and upgraded the feedback questionnaires. Furthermore, the evaluators observed some of the program activities, such as a workshop designed to empower the participants and impart skills for job search. Periodically, the evaluation findings were presented and discussed at the policy makers' forums, such as the steering committee of the project, composed of stakeholders from various governmental bodies.

Learning about the program on the basis of systematic analysis of a variety of data sources and diverse perspectives allowed us to understand the needs and wishes of different stakeholders. Conducting informal conversations with the participants in the course of observing the project's activities and facilitating focus groups with the staff helped to build cooperative evaluator–evaluee relationships. We also initiated periodic updating meetings with the program director and the coordinator to monitor program implementation processes, thereby learning in real time about the pertinent issues engaging the staff. Moreover, we held periodic meetings with the project staff who were devoted to in-depth discussion of a specific query each time, such as definitions of success. Another instance of promoting a genuine partnership was a discourse addressing the overall design of the program's work procedures, which emerged largely from the cumulative experiences of the staff members. This task served as an input for developing strategic plans to promote the project's sustainability. A similar focus group technique was used to develop an information management system (MIS) to support the follow-up of the project and encourage continuous learning.

In a similar vein, we initiated discussions with the participants, attempting to grasp their perceptions of the program goals, operations, and other issues of concern. For instance, parallel to the focus group with the staff addressing definitions of program success, a workshop was organized for the participants where the same issue was discussed from their perspective. The workshop was designed by the professional director in cooperation with the evaluation team, utilizing the expertise of both partners: The professional director facilitated the workshop, and the evaluators documented it and analyzed the emerging findings. This was a manifestation of the structural element of genuine partnership building: division of tasks in accordance with the partners' specialties, which enhances power balancing.

Overall, the design and conduct of meetings with the program staff and the participants reflected the four elements of building genuine partnership: (1) negotiation (discussions of core issues such as definition of success, work procedures, strategic plans), (2) coordination (periodical updating meetings), (3) power balancing (meetings of the evaluators with evaluees on a cooperative basis), and (4) reflection and learning (jointly designing MIS to support learning).

Thus, aside from the substantive goals of the meetings, the fundamental goal of building genuine evaluator–evaluee partnership was ever-present. This aim was based on a joint motivation to advance a shared goal of promoting social justice for the program participants—creating equal job opportunities for the learning-disabled. Creating synergy between knowledge based on practice with the systematic data collection and analysis underscored by the evaluation team enhanced the program operations and expression of genuine voices by different partners while interacting with multiple stakeholders, each embracing a distinct professional orientation (Desivilya Syna & Palgi, 2011).

Conclusions: The Role of Evaluation in Fostering Social Justice

This article presented an evaluation model carrying the potential to foster social justice for a vulnerable population. The framework integrated the changing relationship view of evaluation and the notion of genuine partnership (Abma & Widdershoven, 2008; Desivilya Syna & Palgi, 2011). It was illustrated by the evaluation of a program supporting college graduates with learning disabilities in their transition from college to the job market.

The evaluated project responded to the micro-level individual needs of the learning disabled college graduates identified by special education scholars (Madaus, 2008) and addressed the macro-level—the systemic necessity to counteract the growing inequalities in job-market opportunities, especially salient in the disadvantaged position of vulnerable social groups (Beck, 2000; Bidwell et al., 2013; Stuart et al., 2013). The evaluation model embraces an active stance in an attempt to relay the project's cause and actual accomplishments to policy makers calling for their actions in restoring social justice in the job market. The changing relations view of evaluation and genuine partnership was structured into the logic of the model. Namely, communication of the findings derived from the systematic, ongoing, and collaborative research process, involving the evaluees, can markedly enhance the evaluators' contribution to equal opportunities in the employment arena.

Indeed, the evaluation validated the major assumption of the program: Students with learning disabilities need special support in the transition phase from academic studies to employment. The participants appear aware of the demands placed on job seekers by the competitive job market, underscoring individual responsibility, entrepreneurship and self-presentation, which they perceive as lacking (Madaus, 2008; Stuart et al., 2013). The program has accomplished the task of empowering the participants and imparting relevant job searching skills rather effectively. The project has also made some progress at the macro-level: enhancing employers' awareness regarding learning disabilities and the need to mainstream employees with such characteristics in the job market; building partnerships with employers and other relevant organizations; and follow-up of graduates at their workplaces. Attempts to improve the latter component were addressed in joint evaluator–evaluee forums.

Reflecting upon the insights stemming from the implementation of the social justice in action evaluation model, we can note the following accomplishments:

- In-depth understanding of the needs of the program participants and program staff;
- Ability of evaluators to serve as a sounding board on behalf of the program participants with regard to policy makers;
- Enhanced involvement of the program participants and program staff, creating genuine partnership; and
- Development of a theory of practice through the partnership.

Notwithstanding the strengths, we also encountered two considerable challenges:

- Management of the intricacies of the evaluator–evaluee relationships, especially engaging the complexities of power relations and maintaining the partnership;
- Sustaining the momentum of a "snapshot" evaluation and leveraging its effects on a sociopolitical agenda—fostering equal employment opportunities for vulnerable social groups while not impeding the quality of research and validity of the findings (House, 2014).

Engaging the above challenges and queries paves the way for future learning terrains and research directions.

We would like to conclude by drawing on the argument proposed by the Dardenne brothers, directors of the film *The Kid With a Bike*. They maintained that establishing relationships with others is an essential element in the individual's ability to survive physically and emotionally. They endeavor to prove this contention by means of their cinematographic activities. In a similar vein, we as evaluators presume that social justice cannot be sustained without individuals, professionals, and organizations in all sectors building relationships and forming partnerships.

References

Abma, T., & Widdershoven, A .M. (2008). Evaluation and/as social relation. *Evaluation*, *14*, 209–225.

Beck, U. (2000). *The brave new world of work*. Malden, MA: Polity Press.

Bidwell, M., Briscoe, F., Fernandez-Mateo, I., & Sterling, A. (2013). The employment relationship and inequality: How and why changes in employment practices are shaping rewards in organizations. *The Academy of Management Annals*, *7*(1), 61–121.

Bridgstock, R. (2009). The graduate attributes we've overlooked: Enhancing graduate employability through career management skills. *Higher Education Research & Development*, 28(1), 31–44.

Desivilya Syna, H., & Palgi, M. (2011). Introduction. The nature of partnerships and the processes of their formation: Juxtaposing conflict and cooperation. In H. Desivilya Syna & M. Palgi (Eds.), *The paradox in partnership: The role of conflict in partnership building* (pp. 1–18). Bentham Science e-Books.

Desivilya Syna, H., & Rottman, A. (2012). The role of power asymmetry sensitivity in Jewish–Arab partnerships. *Conflict Resolution Quarterly*, 30(2), 219–241.

Desivilya Syna, H., Rottman, A., & Raz, M. (2014). Partnership among stakeholders as a vehicle for promoting good practices in diversity management: The case of job market integration of college graduates with learning disabilities. In M. Karatas Ozkan, K. Nicolopoulou, & M. F. Ozbilgin (Eds.), *Corporate social responsibility and human resource management: A diversity perspective*. Cheltenham Glos, England: Edward Elgar Publishing.

Doren, B., Lindstrom, L., Zane, C., & Johnson, P. (2007). The role of program and alterable personal factors in postschool employment outcomes. *Career Development for Exceptional Individuals*, 30(3), 171–183.

Fetterman, D. (1994). Empowerment evaluation. *Evaluation Practice*, 15, 1–6.

Greene, J. (2001). Dialogue in evaluation: A relational perspective. *Evaluation*, 7(2), 181–203.

Guba, E. G., & Lincoln, Y. S. (1981). *Effective evaluation*. San Francisco, CA: Jossey-Bass.

House, E. R. (2014). Origins of the ideas in *Evaluating with Validity*. In J. C. Griffith & B. Montrosse-Moorhead (Eds.), *Revisiting truth, beauty, and justice: Evaluating with validity in the 21st century. New Directions for Evaluation*, 142, 9–15.

Lincoln, Y. S. (1993). I and thou: Method, voice, and roles in research with the silenced. In D. McLaughlin & W. Tierney (Eds.), *Naming silenced lives* (pp. 29–47). New York, NY: Routledge.

Madaus, J. W. (2008). Employment self-disclosure rates and rationales of university graduates with learning disabilities. *Journal of Learning Disabilities*, 41(4), 291–299.

Mertens, D. (2002). The evaluator's role in the transformative context. In K. E. Ryan & T. S. Schwandt (Eds.), *Exploring evaluator role and identity* (pp. 17–36). Greenwich, CT: IAP.

Moreau, M. P., & Leathwood, C. (2006). Graduates' employment and the discourse of employability: A critical analysis. *Journal of Education and Work*, 19(4), 305–324.

Parlett, M., & Hamilton, D. (1972). Evaluation as illumination: A new approach to the study of innovatory programs. In G. Glass (Ed.), *Evaluation review studies annual 1*, pp. 140–157. Beverly Hills, CA: SAGE.

Patton, M. Q. (1997). *Utilization-focused evaluation: New century edition*. Thousand Oaks, CA: SAGE.

Rawls, J. (1999). *A theory of justice* (rev. ed.). Cambridge, MA: Belknap Press of Harvard University Press.

Scriven, M. (1997). Truth and objectivity in evaluation. In E. Chelimsky & W. R. Shadish (Eds.), *Evaluation for the 21st century: A handbook* (pp. 477–500). Thousand Oaks, CA: SAGE.

Stake, R. E. (1991). Retrospective on "The countenance of educational evaluation." In M. W. McLaughlin & D. C. Philips (Eds.), *Evaluation and education: A quarter century: Ninetieth yearbook of the National Society for the Study of Education* (pp. 67–88). Chicago, IL: NSSE and University of Chicago Press.

Stuart, M., Grugulis, I., Tomlinson, J., Forde, C., & MacKenzie, R. (2013). Reflections on work and employment into the 21st century: Between equal rights, force decides. *Work, Employment, and Society*, 27(3), 379–395.

HELENA DESIVILYA SYNA is a professor of social and organizational psychology, currently the chair of the department of MA studies in organizational development and consulting at the Max Stern Yezreel Valley College, Israel. She conducts research on social conflict, organizational behavior–interpersonal, intra-group, and intergroup relations, and diversity management (gender, national minorities, people with special needs).

AMIT ROTTMAN is a PhD student in anthropology of education, University of Haifa, Israel, and specializes in the areas of social class and schooling, diversity in intergroup relations, and qualitative research.

MICHAL RAZ is a PhD student in the Swiss Center for Conflict Research, Management and Resolution, the Hebrew University in Jerusalem, Israel, and specializes in organizational sociology, diversity management, social conflict, research methods, and statistics.

Gruskin, S., Waller, E., Safreed-Harmon, K., Ezer, T., Cohen, J., Gathumbi, A. & Kameri-Mbote, P. (2015). Integrating human rights in program evaluation: Lessons from law and health programs in Kenya. In B. Rosenstein & H. Desivilya Syna (Eds.), *Evaluation and social justice in complex sociopolitical contexts. New Directions for Evaluation, 146,* 57–69.

5

Integrating Human Rights in Program Evaluation: Lessons From Law and Health Programs in Kenya

Sofia Gruskin, Emily Waller, Kelly Safreed-Harmon, Tamar Ezer, Jonathan Cohen, Anne Gathumbi, Patricia Kameri-Mbote

Abstract

Methods for assessing both the inclusion and impact of human rights within health program design and implementation are still nascent. We used human rights concepts and methods to evaluate the programs of three Kenyan nongovernmental organizations that integrate legal and health services as a means to empower key populations to better understand and claim their rights and improve their access to health care and justice. Drawing on evaluation experiences and results, this paper demonstrates that the systematic application of human rights principles and strategies can support the conceptualization of monitoring and evaluation objectives through logic model design, the identification and selection of appropriate evaluation measures, and the analysis of evaluation data. This evaluation represents an important step in moving human rights–related evaluation work beyond the mere conceptual and into the operational. © 2015 Wiley Periodicals, Inc., and the American Evaluation Association.

T he promotion and protection of human rights is widely noted as key to an effective HIV/AIDS response and to public health efforts more generally. In light of this dynamic, three Kenyan nongovernmental organizations (NGOs) utilized support from the Open Society Foundations (OSF) to integrate legal services into existing health services addressing gender-based violence and general HIV clinical care, with the ultimate aim of supporting the health and human rights of key populations.

In Kenya, as elsewhere, people living with HIV (PLHIV), survivors of gender-based violence, and women and children more generally experience human rights violations that undermine their health and quality of life. A 2008 report by the Institute of Development Studies documented a high level of violence against women in Kenya and emphasized that despite much demand, the availability of and funding for violence rehabilitation, accountability mechanisms, and appropriate medical care remained sparse (Crichton, Musembi, & Ngugi, 2008). Moreover, an assessment of legal services for PLHIV in Kenya indicated that human rights abuses, including sexual violence, stigma, and discrimination, fuel the HIV epidemic, especially among socially marginalized groups, and that access to affordable legal services is extremely limited (Kalla & Cohen, 2007).

Addressing this situation through programs that integrate legal and health services (hereafter "legal integration programs") is a strategy suggested by other initiatives that have broken new ground in the field of public health (Csete & Cohen, 2010; Ezer, 2008; National Center for Medical-Legal Partnership, n.d.). The OSF initiative established legal integration programs within three NGOs: the Christian Health Association of Kenya (CHAK), the Coalition on Violence Against Women (COVAW), and the Legal Aid Centre of Eldoret (LACE).

CHAK is a faith-based organization that operates more than 400 Kenyan health facilities and provides a broad range of HIV prevention and treatment services. In its legal integration program, CHAK trained health providers and community representatives of PLHIV to incorporate law and human rights into community outreach activities and support group meetings in several of its health facilities. CHAK also sensitized community leaders about human rights and partnered with local legal aid organizations.

COVAW is a national women's human rights organization focusing on violence against women, including how violence against women intersects with HIV. COVAW integrated health and legal services for survivors

We would like to extend our deepest thanks to the Christian Health Association of Kenya (CHAK), the Coalition on Violence Against Women (COVAW), and the Legal Aid Centre of Eldoret (LACE) for their engagement and participation in this evaluation. Many thanks to Wilson Kamande, Yvette Efevbera, and Laura Ferguson for their assistance at different phases of this project. We wish in particular to acknowledge the import contribution of Zyde Raad at every stage of this research project, and to earlier versions of this article. And finally, thanks to Open Society Foundations for its generous support of this evaluation.

of gender-based violence at post-rape centers in a large referral hospital and a smaller district hospital in Nairobi. Activities included providing legal aid, training health care providers, and implementing a pro bono legal scheme.

LACE was founded by Kenyan attorneys and judges to represent people who otherwise have limited access to justice, particularly PLHIV. LACE established a legal aid office as part of the United States Agency for International Development—Academic Model Providing Access to Healthcare (AMPATH) site in Eldoret, a city northwest of the capital of Nairobi. The program provided comprehensive care and treatment to PLHIV. PLHIV with otherwise limited access to justice received training, direct legal representation, and referrals to pro bono services.

Findings discussed in this paper, and published separately, point to legal integration activities being associated with a number of desirable outcomes with implications for health and well-being. These included the provision of legal aid to clients, referrals to other needed resources, and training of groups of clients and health care providers on legal and human rights issues (Gruskin et al., 2013). Discrimination, land and property ownership, housing, child support, and sexual and gender-based violence were all issues that clients commonly addressed through the legal integration programs. It is estimated that the three legal integration programs collectively delivered services to more than 500 individual clients in the time period covered by this evaluation.

This evaluation experience notably provides insight into the potential contributions of human rights paradigms to evaluation science. Developing and implementing the evaluation protocol and instruments suggest a number of issues that may be relevant to others seeking to address social justice issues through evaluation, and is synergistic with growing recognition of the need to measure the impact of human rights–based programs and how to apply human rights concepts in evaluation (World Health Organization, 2013). Building this knowledge base will contribute more generally to clarifying the role of evaluation in promoting social justice, in part by calling attention to inequalities and power imbalances among social groups.

Evaluation Background

Human rights concepts and methods have been used to improve health processes and outcomes worldwide through advocacy, through use of the courts, and in health programming. A widely recognized tenet in much of this work is that health outcomes can be linked via causal pathways to underlying factors in the physical and social environment such as those relating to an individual's housing, educational opportunities, income-generating opportunities, and experiences of discrimination. Notably, these underlying factors also are manifestations of the realization or denial of human rights such as the rights to housing, education, an adequate standard of living, and freedom from discrimination (Baral et al., 2009).

In other words, advancing an individual's right to education, for example, can be not only an end in itself but also a means of advancing that same individual's right to health. Therefore, while some health and human rights initiatives focus only on aspects of health systems or health services, others seek to improve health outcomes primarily through non-health pathways (Pronyk et al., 2006).

In the legal integration programs that were the focus of our evaluation, clients brought forth issues with extensive implications for health and well-being. Helping a client whose HIV-positive status was the basis for termination from a job was understood to advance that person's right to health, illustrating the demonstrated correlation between financial status and health status (Commission on Social Determinants of Health, 2008). The legal integration programs were integrated into conventional health programming, but the focus of this evaluation was strictly the value of the legal integration programs in and of themselves.

Public health leaders and practitioners recognize the elements of what is termed a human rights–based approach (HRBA) and how this approach can strengthen the effectiveness of public health programming (Gruskin, Bogecho, & Ferguson, 2010). Key human rights definitions and concepts agreed upon by evaluators at the outset of this evaluation process are presented in Table 5.1.

Despite the potential of human rights to inform health policies and programs, evaluation methods and indicators that specifically capture human rights concerns are not well developed and those that exist are often used inconsistently (Gruskin & Ferguson, 2009). International health and development organizations that have been applying human rights–based approaches to the design and implementation of programs are increasingly interested in monitoring and evaluating the impact of this work (International Center for Research on Women, n.d.; Oxfam America & CARE USA, 2007). The World Health Organization recently assessed governmental efforts to improve women's and children's health through various rights-based interventions and found evidence of health-related gains (World Health Organization, 2013).

Within this context, the evaluation of the Kenyan legal integration programs sought to: (a) assess program achievements, including those related to human rights concepts such as empowerment and nondiscrimination, and (b) examine whether integrating human rights norms and standards improved the delivery of services. An important benefit has been to shed light on the experiences of disenfranchised people in different types of settings within Kenya. Kenyatta National Hospital, the site of the COVAW legal integration activities that were evaluated, is one of Kenya's largest public hospitals. As such, it serves a broad cross-section of Nairobi's poorest residents. Many of the LACE program's clients similarly were referred by

Table 5.1. Key Human Rights Definitions and Concepts Utilized for the Evaluation

Human rights	Human rights are universal legal guarantees enshrined in international human rights treaties that create legally binding obligations on the nations that ratify them and have the status and power of international law. International human rights law is about defining what governments can do to us, cannot do to us, and should do for us (Office of the United Nations High Commissioner for Human Rights, n.d.).
Rights-based approach to health	A rights-based approach to health is explicitly shaped by human rights principles, including attention to the key elements of the right to health; participation; equality, and nondiscrimination; the legal and policy context; and accountability (Gruskin, Bogecho, & Ferguson, 2010).
Key elements of the right to health: (3AQ)	As stated in General Comment 14 of the UN Committee on Economic, Social, and Cultural Rights, a state's obligations under the right to health include ensuring the availability, accessibility, acceptability, and quality of health facilities, goods, and services (Committee on Economic, Social and Cultural Rights, 2000).
	Availability: Functioning public health and healthcare facilities, goods, and services, as well as programs, have to be available in sufficient quantity. The precise nature of the facilities, goods, and services will vary depending on numerous factors, including the level of development within the society.
	Accessibility: Accessibility has four overlapping dimensions: nondiscrimination; physical accessibility; economic accessibility (affordability); and information accessibility.
	Acceptability: All health facilities, goods, and services must be respectful of medical ethics and culturally appropriate, that is, respectful of the culture of individuals, minorities, peoples, and communities; sensitive to gender and life-cycle requirements; and designed to respect confidentiality and improve the health status of those concerned.
	Quality: Health facilities, goods, and services must be scientifically and medically appropriate and of good quality (Committee on Economic, Social and Cultural Rights, 2000).
Participation	The right of individuals and groups to participate in decision-making processes is an integral component of any policy, program or strategy developed to discharge governmental obligations under the right to health. Promoting health thus involves effective community action in setting priorities, making decisions, and planning, implementing, and evaluating (Gruskin, Bogecho, & Ferguson, 2010).

(Continued)

NEW DIRECTIONS FOR EVALUATION • DOI: 10.1002/ev

Table 5.1. Continued

Equality and nondiscrimination	Any discrimination in access to health care and the underlying determinants of health is proscribed, as well as to the means and entitlements for their procurement, on the grounds of race, color, sex, language, religion, political or other opinion, national or social origin, property, birth, physical or mental disability, health status (including HIV/AIDS), sexual orientation and civil, political, social or other status, (Committee on Economic, Social and Cultural Rights, 2000).
Accountability	Governments are accountable to their populations and to the international community for their actions which impact on health and development. Accountability mechanisms should exist at local, national, regional, and international levels to monitor compliance and support governments in fulfilling their human rights obligations. Any person or group victim of a health-related violation should have access to effective judicial or other appropriate remedies at all levels. All victims of such violations should be entitled to adequate reparation, in the form of restitution, compensation, satisfaction or guarantees of non-repetition (Schrecker, Chapman, Labonté, & De Vogli, 2010).

Source: Adapted from Gruskin et al. (2012).

an HIV clinic that seeks to make health services accessible to poor residents of Eldoret, a city of 300,000 people near Kenya's western border with Uganda. Both of the CHAK evaluation sites are health clinics with large caseloads of patients who lack the resources to pay out-of-pocket for health care: one in Mombasa, a major commercial center on Kenya's east coast, and one in Naivasha, a rural agricultural community 90 kilometers northwest of Nairobi.

Evaluation Overview

We assessed legal aid interventions aimed at improving health services and underlying determinants of health such as access to employment and education. A logic model was created by identifying legal integration activities, outcomes, and human rights principles relevant to the work of each organization. We identified quantitative and qualitative methods to capture each structure, process, and outcome component of the logic model. We then integrated human rights principles such as participation, non-discrimination, accountability, and empowerment into all instruments developed [instruments available upon request].

Data collection for the evaluation took place in 2010–2011. Data were collected through meetings, site visits, interviews, and focus group discussions with the organizations' legal and health staff, patients, and clients. The organizations' existing client records and other routine data were obtained to calculate quantitative and outcome indicators of onsite legal service provision, referrals, and case outcomes.

Client records were entered into a database and quantified to capture indicators of interest. Data from the questionnaire, case review worksheets, and interview and focus group discussion transcripts were entered into qualitative analysis software (NVivo 9). A qualitative analysis plan was established. Thematic content analysis was used to code data, focusing on the generation of key words, phrases, and themes concerning programming, legal and human rights issues, and the HRBA elements from the logic model. Comparisons were drawn between control and intervention groups of clients and staff where possible.

Incorporation of Human Rights Into the Evaluation

Human rights were systematically applied to support evaluation objectives through the logic model design, the identification and selection of appropriate measures, and the analysis of evaluation data, as described in the following subsections. The inclusion of human rights principles in the evaluation process provided a vehicle to promote social justice not only through programming objectives but also in relation to how the value of the projects was assessed.

Human Rights in Logic Model Development

Logic models, commonly used in health programming to understand associations between program activities and objectives, assess assumptions underlying change, and elucidate programming strengths and weaknesses (Affi, Makhoul, El Hajj, & Nakkash, 2011; Hawkins, Clinton-Sherrod, Irvin, Hart, & Russell, 2009; Holliman, 2010). They are seen as particularly useful for program monitoring and evaluation (W. K. Kellogg Foundation, 2000).

We developed our logic model by combining a conventional structure-process-outcome-impact evaluation framework with elements commonly understood to form part of a human rights–based approach to programming. Figure 5.1 depicts the logic model used for the evaluation. The structure components are based on resources employed by the three NGOs in their legal integration work. The process components are based on common organizational activities to integrate legal support into their health services. Program outcomes relate to health and the underlying determinants of health for people living with and affected by HIV and gender-based violence. Drawing on the UN Common Understanding of a Human Rights–Based Approach (United Nations, 2003), impact was defined as building the capacity of rights-holders and duty-bearers to claim and fulfill rights.

Figure 5.1. Human Rights in Logic Model Development

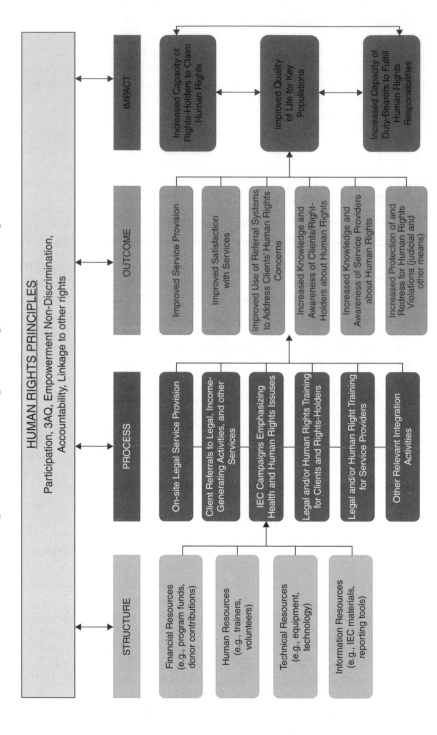

Note: IEC = information, education, and communication.
3AQ = availability, accessibility, acceptability, and quality of services (the core components of the right to health).

In developing the logic model, we identified human rights principles deemed common and relevant to all three legal integration programs and their programming objectives. These included: five elements of a human rights–based approach to programming (participation, accountability, nondiscrimination, empowerment, and linkage to other rights) (Open Society Institute and Equites, 2009; United Nations, 2003); the core components of the right to health; and rights relating to information, education, an adequate standard of living, justice, and security of person. Attention to these rights and principles was ensured by conceptualizing measurable processes and outcomes to capture both programming goals and human rights dimensions.

Using Human Rights to Shape Evaluation Instruments

We integrated human rights and rights-related principles into the development of qualitative protocols and the selection of quantitative indicators for measuring processes and outcomes.

Rights concepts were addressed in qualitative work through direct questions, follow-up questions, and probes. For example, some interview protocols contained questions directly related to the principle of participation, including questions about how communities were involved in the planning and implementation of trainings.

Some quantitative indicators were specifically selected to capture human rights-relevant information, such as the proportion of clients receiving legal referrals or cases resolved through community mechanisms. Indicators were then coded for the human rights elements they reflected, in particular the 3AQ (see Table 5.1). For example, the proportion of clients receiving help with legal documents over a specified period is related to the human rights principle of empowerment and to the availability and accessibility of services. When disaggregated by sex, age, and other relevant categories, it can also capture discrimination and inequalities. Thus, social justice for particular groups was promoted throughout the evaluation process.

Capturing Human Rights in Data Analysis

We applied traditional qualitative analysis techniques to capture human rights and programming dynamics and outcomes. The analysis was organized into two coding sections with explicit attention to rights.

Based on the conceptual logic model, the first section focused on a tiered structure of data analysis with attention to human rights principles, norms, and standards: for example, differentiating human rights training of health and/or legal service providers versus clients who had received services. The second coding section captured emerging concepts and themes, related to but beyond the specific focus of the evaluation, such as in relation to "gender," "vulnerable populations," and "advocacy."

Systematic attention to human rights in data analysis brought to light important findings, including patterns within and across programs. One such example is the powerful role of informal community mechanisms, like village elders, chiefs, and assistant chiefs, in resolving noncriminal legal conflicts (for example, loss of property and disinheritance). Findings also revealed successes in using alternative dispute resolution, for example, to help clients resolve housing problems and to obtain children's school fees. Clients used formal legal channels as well, with the programs assisting in both criminal and civil cases. Legal and human rights training was an important area of activity for all programs.

Qualitative findings provide insight into how these activities were perceived by clients and providers as advancing human rights and improving underlying determinants of health, including food, shelter and education. Because of the attention given to the right to information and the principle of empowerment, the data analysis helped to qualitatively document improvements in knowledge and awareness of human rights among clients and service providers who participated in legal integration programs. For example, as compared to control groups of untrained clients, trained clients showed a more detailed conceptual knowledge of human rights and a better understanding of how to claim rights.

Challenges and Limitations

Several challenges emerged during this evaluation. The different perspectives and priorities of the research team members, program staff, and funders were particularly important. For example, while the primary intent of the research team was to develop a robust interdisciplinary evaluation methodology, the funder's main focus was to determine whether program outcomes had been achieved, and program staff sought to ensure that their work would continue to be funded. Navigating the conceptual differences and vested interests of all actors was necessary in order to reach a common understanding about both the process and the outcomes of the evaluation.

Lack of quality routine data collected by the NGOs posed significant limitations. Simple changes in routine monitoring systems could have ensured more systematic attention to a range of human rights. For instance, routinely collecting client data on gender, age, and ethnicity could have enabled disaggregation to investigate whether certain populations were utilizing the services on offer to a lesser extent than others.

The lack of control groups and the small size of some of the focus group discussions and small number of interviews also posed limitations, underscoring the importance of considering contextual factors when designing evaluations, especially the capacity of program staff to support evaluations being undertaken within small grassroots initiatives (Habicht, Victora, & Vaughan, 1999; Victora, Habicht, & Bryce, 2004).

Conclusion

This evaluation experience highlighted important entry points for building the evidence base regarding the added value of using human rights and rights-based approaches to affect underlying determinants of health such as educational attainment, freedom from discrimination, and access to justice.

Incorporation of human rights within the logic model illustrated three important issues. First, rights can be systematically integrated into the conceptualization and definition of processes, outcomes, and impacts. Second, rights can serve as a tool to analyze linkages in a logic model, and it is possible to document how rights principles might be operating implicitly or indirectly within legal integration programs. Third, human rights can provide a strong foundation for assessing the link between rights and programming objectives in subsequent evaluation steps, including data analysis.

The approach piloted here may be especially valuable in settings where complex obstacles need to be addressed in order for marginalized populations to achieve social justice. More work is needed to increase the feasibility of combining human rights and conventional evaluation approaches, especially for small and under-resourced programs. This evaluation represents an important step in moving human rights–related evaluation work forward.

References

Afifi, R. A., Makhoul, J., El Hajj, T., & Nakkash, R. T. (2011). Developing a logic model for youth mental health: Participatory research with a refugee community in Beirut. *Health Policy and Planning*, 26(6), 508–517.

Baral, S., Trapence, G., Motimedi, F., Umar, E., Iipinge, S., Dausab, F., & Beyrer, C. (2009, March 26). HIV prevalence, risks for HIV infection, and human rights among men who have sex with men (MSM) in Malawi, Namibia, and Botswana. *PLoS ONE*, 4(3), e4997 (e-publication).

Commission on Social Determinants of Health. (2008). *Closing the gap in a generation: Health equity through action on the social determinants of health: Final report of the Commission on Social Determinants of Health.* Retrieved from http://www.who.int /social_determinants/final_report/en

Committee on Economic, Social, and Cultural Rights. (2000). The right to the highest attainable standard of health: 11/08/2000. E/C.12/2000/4, CESCR General Comment 14. Twenty-second session Geneva, 25 April–12 May 2000, Agenda item 3.

Crichton, J., Musembi, C. N., & Ngugi, A. (2008). *Painful tradeoffs: Intimate-partner violence and sexual and reproductive health rights in Kenya* (Institute of Development Studies Working Paper 312).

Csete, J., & Cohen, J. (2010). Health benefits of legal services for criminalized population: The case of people who use drugs, sex workers and sexual and gender minorities. *The Journal of Law, Medicine, & Ethics*, 38(4), 816–831.

Ezer, T. (2008). Lessons from Africa: Combating the twin epidemics of domestic violence and HIV/AIDS. *HIV/AIDS Policy Law Review, 13*, 57–62.

Gruskin, S., Ahmed, S., Bogecho, D., Ferguson, L., Hanefeld, J., MacCarthy, S., Raad, Z., & Steiner, R. (2012). Human rights in health systems frameworks: What is there, what is missing, and why does it matter? *Global Public Health, 7*(4), 337–351.

Gruskin, S., Bogecho, D., & Ferguson, L. (2010). Rights-based approaches to health policies and programmes: Articulations, ambiguities and assessment. *Journal of Public Health Policy, 31*(2), 129–145.

Gruskin, S., & Ferguson, L. (2009). Using indicators to determine the contribution of human rights to public health efforts. *Bulletin of the World Health Organization, 87*(9), 714–719.

Gruskin, S., Safreed-Harmon, K., Ezer, T., Gathumbi, A., Cohen, J., & Kameri-Mbote, P. (2013). Access to justice: Evaluating law, health and human rights programmes in Kenya. *Journal of the International AIDS Society, 16*(suppl 2), 18726.

Habicht, J. P., Victora, C. G., & Vaughan J. P. (1999). Evaluation designs for adequacy, plausibility and probability of public health programme performance and impact. *International Journal of Epidemiology, 28*(1), 10–18.

Hallinan, C. M. (2010). Program logic: A framework for health program design and evaluation—the Pap nurse in general practice program. *Australian Journal of Primary Health, 16*(4), 319–325.

Hawkins, S. R., Clinton-Sherrod, A. M., Irvin, N., Hart, L., & Russell, S. J. (2009). Logic models as a tool for sexual violence prevention program development. *Health Promotion Practice, 10*, 29S–37S.

International Center for Research on Women. (n.d.). *Insight into action: Gender and property rights.* Retrieved from http://www.icrw.org/events/insight-action-gender -and-property-rights

Kalla, K., & Cohen, J. (2007). *Ensuring justice for vulnerable communities in Kenya: A review of HIV and AIDS-related legal services.* New York, NY: Open Society Institute.

National Center for Medical–Legal Partnership. (n.d.). Retrieved from http://www .medical-legalpartnership.org

Office of the United Nations High Commissioner for Human Rights. (n.d.). What are human rights? [online]. Retrieved from http://www.ohchr.org/EN/Issues/Pages /WhatareHumanRights.aspx

Open Society Institute & Equitas International Centre for Human Rights Education. (2009). *Health and human rights—A resource guide.* Retrieved from http://hhrguide .org/

Oxfam America & CARE USA. (2007). *Rights-based approaches: Learning project.* Boston, MA: Oxfam America.

Pronyk, P. M., Hargreaves, J. R., Kim, J. C., Morison, L. A., Phetla, G., Watts, C., Busza, J., & Porter, J. D. H. (2006). Effect of a structural intervention for the prevention of intimate-partner violence and HIV in rural South Africa: A cluster randomised trial. *Lancet, 368*(9551), 1973–1983.

Schrecker, T., Chapman, A. R., Labonté, R., & De Vogli, R. (2010). Advancing health equity in the global marketplace: how human rights can help. *Social Science and Medicine, 71*(8), 1520–1526.

United Nations. (1966). International Covenant on Economic, Social and Cultural Rights (ICESCR).

United Nations. (2003). *The human rights–based approach to development cooperation towards a common understanding among the UN agencies ("Common Understanding").* Retrieved from http://hrbaportal.org/the-human-rights-based-approach-to-development -cooperation-towards-a-common-understanding-among-un-agencies

Victora, C. G., Habicht, J. P., & Bryce, J. (2004). Evidence-based public health: Moving beyond randomized trials. *American Journal of Public Health, 94*(3), 400–405.

W. K. Kellogg Foundation. (2000). *Using logic models to bring together planning, evaluation & action: Logic model development guide.* Battle Creek, MI: W. K. Kellogg Foundation.

World Health Organization. (2013). *Women's and children's health: Evidence of impact of human rights.* Retrieved from http://www.who.int/maternal_child_adolescent /documents/women_children_human_rights/en/

SOFIA GRUSKIN is a professor at the Keck School of Medicine and the Gould School of Law, and the director of the Program on Global Health and Human Rights, Institute for Global Health, at the University of Southern California.

EMILY WALLER is a doctoral researcher in the School of Social Sciences at the University of New South Wales, Sydney, Australia.

KELLY SAFREED-HARMON is an independent consultant affiliated with the Program on Global Health and Human Rights, Institute for Global Health, University of Southern California.

TAMAR EZER is the deputy director of the Law and Health Initiative of the Open Society Public Health Program.

JONATHAN COHEN is the deputy director of the Open Society Public Health Program.

ANNE GATHUMBI is the director of the Sexual Health and Rights Project at the Open Society Public Health Program.

PATRICIA KAMERI-MBOTE is the founding research director at the International Environmental Law Research Centre at Strathmore University, Nairobi, Kenya.

NEW DIRECTIONS FOR EVALUATION • DOI: 10.1002/ev

Zamir, J., & Abu Jaber, S. (2015). Promoting social justice through a new teacher training pro-
gram for the Bedouin population in the Negev: An evaluation case study. In B. Rosenstein
& H. Desivilya Syna (Eds.), *Evaluation and social justice in complex sociopolitical contexts.*
New Directions for Evaluation, 146, 71–82.

6

Promoting Social Justice Through a New Teacher Training Program for the Bedouin Population in the Negev: An Evaluation Case Study

Judith Zamir, Saleem Abu Jaber

Abstract

*This article presents the changes that took place in a new training model for stu-
dent teachers in the Bedouin population as a result of joint work with the Evaluation Department and the Training Team of Kaye College for Education from the
beginning of the program. The cooperation between the evaluation team and the
program developers promoted equal opportunities for the Bedouin women teachers involved in the program. The joint project lasted for three years. Throughout
this period, the evaluation department contributed to program development by
means of developmental evaluation. The results show a higher quality of teacher
training, including the enrichment of practicum at schools, the development of
team and students' social commitment and belonging, and the empowerment of
women by improving their status at the professional and community level. The
sense of independence and self-confidence acquired by Bedouin women participating in the program constitutes a small and central step on the way toward
social justice.* © 2015 Wiley Periodicals, Inc., and the American Evaluation
Association.

T he Bedouin population in the Negev (in the south of Israel) continues to encounter logistic and cultural challenges. It is particularly true in relation to teacher-training programs. One of the difficulties involves transportation to the school where students conduct their practicum. Another is that some Bedouin families are reluctant to allow female students to travel from one Bedouin village to another.

The Bedouin population is a society in transition. On one hand, mobility has increased, higher educational opportunities are available, and exposure to the world outside the community has grown. On the other hand, these changes have led to a resurgence of conservatism and religious fundamentalism.

The Kaye College team, under the leadership of Dr. Saleem Abu Jaber, designed a pioneer model of four Partner Development Schools (PDS) based on known models (Goodlad, 1987) focusing on geographic, social, and cultural needs. These adjustments were accommodated in three geographical axes, thus enabling the students to reach the schools for their practicum and to get there on time.

We will present:

1. The characteristics of Bedouin society in transition
2. The new program design
3. The way in which the program was monitored by the evaluation unit and how this follow-up fostered equal opportunities for Bedouin future teachers thus promoting social inclusion and social justice
4. The changes made in the program as a response to field needs and to the evaluation recommendations

The Bedouin Community in the Negev[1]

The Negev Bedouin community is a traditional Muslim society and an integral part of the Arab-Palestinian minority in Israel. Over seventy thousand Bedouins resided in the Negev before 1948. After the establishment of the State of Israel in 1948, only 12,000 remained (Marks, 1974). Since the late 1960s, this community has been undergoing an urbanization process initiated by the Israeli government, a process of moving from a seminomadic lifestyle to living in urban settlements. Today, the Bedouin population consists of more than 200,000 people, 80,000 of whom reside in "the unrecognized villages" (Gradus & Abu-Bader, 2011). About half of the populations live in seven permanent urban townships, all of which are on the bottom of the socioeconomic scale of Israeli towns (Gradus & Abu-Bader, 2011). Living conditions in the unrecognized villages are among the worst in Israel, with inferior infrastructures of running water, electricity, roads, health, education, and welfare services (Swirsky & Hasson, 2005). The events of 1948 and the forceful implementation of the urbanization process between the

1960s and the 1990s harmed the norms and values of ancient traditions in a way that was perceived by many as interfering with the social life structure of the Bedouin population as a tribal society and with its conventions.

Adjustment to the semiurban lifestyle is difficult both socially and economically when there is no parallel investment and development by the authorities to find economical alternatives. Moreover, the traditional leadership was replaced by the leadership of the local municipalities. This has led to deep fractures in the traditional tribal system that influences the family unit, the economic status, and educational and political conditions (Abu Saad, Lithwick, & Abu Saad, 2004; Meir & Barnea, 1986).

The urbanization process requires the redefinition of social relations. Bedouin who have moved into the towns are far more exposed to Israeli and Western influences than ever before, especially to the rise in the cost of living and the transition of children and women from the status of *producers* to *consumers* (Gruber, 1989). To this day, expanding employment possibilities and raising the salary levels among Bedouin workers are perceived as essential for reconciling this conflict (Abu Saad, 2008).

The Status of Women in Bedouin Society

Studies of traditional societies in the world, especially in the Arab-Muslim world (Ariel, 1984; El Saudi, 1988), claim that the gap between the status of women and men has remained the same, while over the past 20 years it has, in fact, been changing in a minor way. This is true to a great extent about Bedouin society in the Negev as well. The public domain is dominated by men, and women have had no part in external public issues (Fenster, 1999), but rather are actively involved in decision making and influencing the family domain. Women's honor plays a great part in their lives, and harming that honor is considered harm to the whole family and tribe. The same is true about Arab women in Israeli society.

Many changes have occurred in the Bedouin way of life with the move from encampments to townships. These include a rise in the cost of living, population density and friction in the tribal sphere. These changes have especially influenced the lives of women. Erosion of her socioeconomic status has brought about greater scrutiny regarding the appearance of the Bedouin woman, together with a need for redefinition of different elements of gender relations (Abu Saad, 2008).

Over the past decades (beginning in the 1980s), several opportunities have become available for young girls to study with boys in mixed classrooms (mainly in Kaye College in Beer Sheva and Achva college near Kiryat Malachi), leading to the formation of relationships outside the family boundaries. Some women have now begun university studies. This exposure to the outside world (outside of the house, the family, and the community) still presents many difficulties that are not due to the family or tribe.

Israeli government policies since the establishment of the State have made it difficult for Bedouin women to develop and integrate into modern Israeli society. These policies have manifested mainly in the issues of land—the unrecognized villages—and they make it very hard for Bedouin women to be mobile in their immediate environs and the surrounding area. In many cases, the infrastructures, transport, and public transportation prevent them from integrating in the academic life in colleges and universities, such as Kaye College and Ben-Gurion University. Nevertheless, several studies (Abu-Rabia Queder, 2007; Tal, 1995) point to changes in the status of Bedouin women, especially during the past two decades, in social, economic, and educational domains. More and more girls finish their high school education and go on to study in institutions for higher education, especially in teacher training colleges such as Kaye, Sapir, and Achva Colleges.

The first organized framework for training Bedouin teachers in Israel was established in 1975 in a teachers' and kindergarten teachers' training seminar in Beer Sheva, today's Kaye College. The beginning of this framework was a special classroom for Bedouin students that opened with 22 students, only one of whom was female—Nayef Abu Siam, from the town of Rahat. This woman paved the way for thousands of Bedouin women to acquire a higher education.

The New Program Design

Kaye College is the locale of the case presented here. The fact that the evaluation unit joined the program team at the very beginning of the program facilitated an interesting process of conceptualization and development. The new model demanded adaptations at the level of the training team. The most significant change was the pedagogic development in the program led by the whole training team. The geographic and cultural adaptations facilitated the process by moving logistic concerns to the sidelines of the program, thus allowing room for pedagogical progress.

The program was designed along three geographical axes: Dimona–Beer Sheva, Arad–Beer Sheva, and Rahat–Beer Sheva (see the map in Figure 6.1), thus giving all students in the area the opportunity to conduct their training in a school near their neighborhoods. This selection reduced the problem around women's mobility.

The team chose to work in a PDS design with four schools participating, thus enriching the training program and reinforcing the practicum (see Figure 6.2). It also developed and expanded professional knowledge in teaching and training. One important question that emerged from the logic model used by the evaluation unit was the team role in relation to the school teachers and the school as a whole. Another important goal of the training team was to build a deep feeling of commitment among school teachers and students.

NEW DIRECTIONS FOR EVALUATION • DOI: 10.1002/ev

Figure 6.1. A Map of the Area Included in the Program

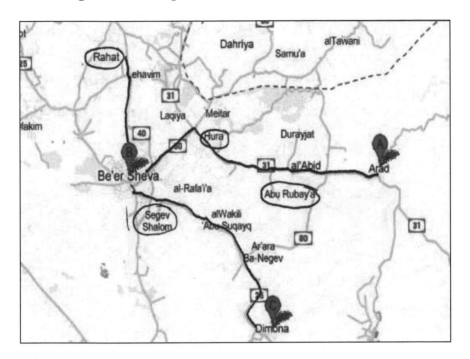

Figure 6.2. Partner Developmental School Design

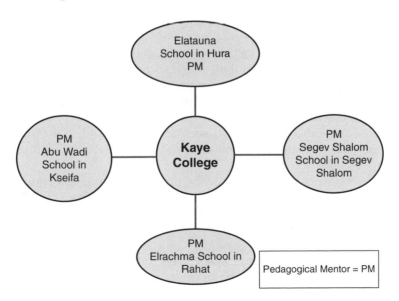

Figure 6.2 illustrates the PDS model. Each participating school has a pedagogical mentor on its staff and a group of second- and third-year student teachers in practicum and contributing to the whole school.

The program aims to:

- Enrich the teachers' training program in the Bedouin population including the practicum at schools
- Develop professional knowledge on training and teaching
- Develop social commitment and belonging
- Empower women by improving their status

The underlying assumption was that an improvement in the socioeconomic status of the Bedouin woman through teacher training would improve her social status within her own community, and open the opportunity for academic development. It would help to crystallize a first step toward social inclusion.

The Evaluation Process and Contribution

Methodology

When the evaluation unit was asked to join the team at the outset, we decided to proceed using Patton's developmental evaluation approach. Developmental evaluation is described by Patton (2011) not as a model, but as a relationship founded on the shared purpose of developing a program. Gamble (2006) relates to developmental evaluation as a way of working, thinking, solving problems, and making changes that fit the changing reality. Developmental evaluation accompanies the whole process of change that takes place in the program, maintaining a flux dialogue with stakeholders, thus reflecting on work and on action (Schon, 1983).

The process of evaluation in the partnership described here was also characterized by special cultural sensitiveness. As described previously, Bedouin society is one in transition from very conservative and authoritarian norms to an open, modern society. On one hand, it aspires to be included in mainstream work markets, and, on the other, it is threatened by the fear of the loss of control.

To be evidence-based and fair, the process of evaluation should take into account every single aspect of the culture that influences the data interpretation. Therefore, the data were collected and interpreted in mixed-cultural teams, giving particular voice to those members coming from within the Bedouin society, both men and women. Furthermore, while Bedouin men perceive Bedouin women as very modern and liberated, the women see themselves as severely oppressed both by Bedouin men and by Israeli society, which marginalizes Bedouin society as a whole. Only a very culturally sensitive evaluation could contribute to the reinforcement and development of the program. There was also a need for feminist method-ologies to help "to construct knowledge without falling into the trap of the patriarchal ways of creating knowledge" (Reinharz, 1992, p. 17).

Starting with the construction of the logic model, most of the data tended to be collected by means of long and repeated observations, in-depth interviews, team meetings, documentation, focus groups, and questionnaires. The key tool for understanding is in the process of data interpretation.

Phase One

As we mentioned in the short description of the program, the PDS was seen by the team as the best suitable solution to the complex picture: lack of suitable transportation from village to village, restriction of women's mobility, late arrival to the practicum at school, and student teacher absence. The result was a very weak and low-level training program, thus reproducing new generations of marginalized groups in Bedouin society and inferior status for female Bedouin teachers.

The construction of the logic model by the team, under the supervision of the evaluation unit, made the goals clear—not only the treatment of student behavioral patterns, but a qualitative, higher level of training as well. The team realized that the initial training had to be more introspective and involve critical thinking on the part of the team members.

As a result, the team engaged in a study program that required its own involvement and commitment. The training team needed to formulate and conduct the evaluation work. The members had to define which goals and activities they wanted examined and recorded. The joint evaluation process and the manner of its implementation furthered the training team's trust in the evaluation staff, resulting in more responsibility on the part of the training team.

The evaluation unit brought a male Bedouin evaluator who could explain cultural codes and motivations to its team. There was also a need for a Bedouin woman on the team to interpret the findings. Accordingly, the Bedouin woman on the training team was consulted several times.

By the end of the first year of work, the team had become an important part of the staff of each school, leading and supervising not only the students, but the teachers as well. In each school, the entire school was becoming more adequately in tune with the demands of modern society. This was regarded by the whole team as a contribution to higher-quality education within Bedouin society.

Phase Two

By the beginning of the second year of the project, the team members had already learned to document the team work by themselves, and the head of the program was assisted in managing developmental issues that emerged from the documented texts.

At the same time, the team asked the evaluation unit to focus on the work with the students rather than on the team work. Therefore, the evaluation unit focused on two issues: (a) examining the team's work together with the head of the program and helping him to lead the team development and skills and (b) interviewing and observing students during their work in the classroom and studying the results.

As a result of this phase, the team was able to refine the definition of the roles and fine-tune them. The evaluation unit found that students were very confused, because many lecturers were present in the schools during practicum and because they did not know how to ask for supervision and from whom. The students were also afraid that misunderstandings could be interpreted by the academic team as insults or disparagement.

The students reinforced the training team by affirming their sense of commitment and belonging to schools. This had been one of the team's main goals.

Phase Three

During the third phase, it was decided to try to help the team by gathering feedback from all the groups affected or influenced by the programs: school principals, school teachers, pupils, and student teachers. As can be seen from Table 6.1, principals, school teachers, and pupils all agreed about the positive influence of the students in the schools regarding teaching and learning processes, school climate, innovation, pupil behavior, and even

Table 6.1. Findings From the Third Year of Work (Collected Data)

Pupils (N = 32)	School teachers (N = 12)	Principals (N = 4)
Mutual support between teachers and students		
Renewal at school through new ways of teaching in classroom, including the use of computers		
Students contributed to a positive social climate in class		
Students help us to understand themes we don't understand in class. They help us to solve problems between friends. They strengthen our self-confidence by teaching us how to express ourselves. When the students are here, the noisy pupils become quiet.	Students bring new ways of teaching. School teachers are experienced in monitoring classes and solving problems, thus contributing to the students' training.	The students contributed to a sense of monitoring and responsibility because the school work becomes transparent.

contribution to pupil self-confidence. The principals stressed the teachers' sense of monitoring and responsibility thanks to the fact that school proceedings became transparent.

Forty-one students filled in questionnaires about the training model design. There were differences in the way they assessed the program during their first year of practicum compared to their experience during the second year:

During the first year of practicum, the mentor and a sense of belonging were central to the positive experience of the practicum.

During the second year of practicum, it was hard to define which variable better predicted a positive experience through practicum. The students were more independent, and there was strong interdependence among different variables, such as a sense of belonging, self-confidence, the relationship with the mentor, and field work.

It is important to stress this outcome within the social context of Bedouin society; the fact that these female students were feeling more independent, self-confident, and professional reflects the achievement of the desired empowerment defined in the program goals.

Changes Made in the Program as a Response to Field Needs and to the Evaluation Recommendations

The partnership between the program developers and the evaluation unit lasted for three years. During this period, the evaluation unit recommended certain changes according to the collected data. The changes that were made as a result of those recommendations are:

- The number of schools and their locations changed from one year to another, due to the changing geographic dispersion of the students, thus introducing an additional dimension of uncertainty and innovation each year.
- During the second year, a fifth school was integrated into the program to provide a special education practicum for students whose training was in this specific field (as recommended by the evaluation team).
- Due to the main focus given to literacy in all schools, a team of mentors and teachers collaborated to professionalize the whole team in literacy.
- The recommendations of the evaluation team during the second and third years showed the need for refining role definitions and making the whole program more known to all the stakeholders from the four schools.

New Directions for Evaluation • DOI: 10.1002/ev

By the end of three years of collaborative work, the evaluation unit recommendations to the program team were:

- Collaborative work in small teams in each classroom (mentor, teacher, and two students) should be supported.
- Students should work to enhance the network on the Internet, and one or more mentors should monitor their work.
- The uniqueness of the program should be redefined.

Conclusions

Developmental evaluation works on situations of high complexity, such as those in early-stage social innovation (Gamble, 2008).

As illustrated by the Panarchy Loop (Westley, Zimmerman, & Patton, 2007), the first phase of work was characterized by a sense of exploration. The training team tried to organize itself randomly. When the program began, it was suddenly clear that each mentor had to cope with a mixed group of students in his school: the second-year students together with the third-year students. Parallel to this challenge, the team began its own series of seminars that led the team to a deeper understanding of members' own expectations of themselves and of the program. The evaluation team had a central role in conducting the logic model, giving feedback online, and conceptualizing the stages.

It should be stressed that in the team of Bedouin mentors, there was one female mentor; the rest were men, one of whom practices traditional polygamy; he is married to two women. Cleary, these male mentors did not fully understand feminist issues. The evaluation team accompanied the exploratory stage, helping to reveal and understand the common goals as well as the discrepancies between staff members, particularly concerning feminist issues.

Toward the second phase, it seemed the program was starting to make sense when the mentors thought that they knew how to define their own roles. Only toward the end of the third stage of work, and with the help of the feedback from all the circles, did the team members begin to redefine their new understandings of the goals and their outcomes. The combination of being evidence-based and objective, together with a role of organizational development coaching, gave the needed balance to the evaluation and facilitated its contribution to the program success (Gamble, 2008).

All the stated goals achieved are the outcome of a process of "conscientization" as Paulo Freire (1998) discussed in his book, *Pedagogy of Freedom*. The teams' awareness of the need for social inclusion led members to work toward enriching the teacher-training program for the Bedouin population, including the practicum at schools, developing professional knowledge about training and teaching, developing social commitment and belonging, and empowering women by improving their status.

Among both the evaluation and the training teams, the sense of partnership and joint commitment provided the vehicle for a small, yet central step on the way toward social justice for Bedouin women in particular, and in the Bedouin community in the field of education in general.

Note

1. From a research proposal submitted by Dr. Nurit Natan et al. to the Research Committee of the Kaye Academic College of Education, August 2013: The influence of studying at Kaye College on the empowerment of Bedouin women in the Negev. The proposal was also submitted to the MOFET Institute, 2014.

References

Abu-Rabi-Queder, S. (2007). Permission to rebel: Arab Bedouin women's changing negotiation of social roles. *Feminist Studies, 33*(1), 161–187.

Abu Saad, A. (2008). ‏הערכה של תכנית לימודים ייחודית בנושאי התורשה, נשואי קרובים ומחלות‎ ‏תורשתיות במגזר הבדואי‎ [Evaluation of a unique study curriculum on the subjects of genetic makeup, inter-familial marriage and hereditary illnesses in the Bedouin sector] (PhD dissertation). Ben-Gurion University of the Negev, Beersheba, Israel.

Abu Saad, I., Lithwick, H., & Abu Saad, K. (2004). *A preliminary evaluation of the Negev Bedouin experience of urbanization.* Negev Center for Regional Development and the Center for Bedouin Studies & Development, Ben Gurion University.

Ariel, M. (1984). ‏בשורת הנשים: האישה המוסלמית - דיכוי במסווה של כבוד המשפחה‎ [The women's message: The Moslem woman—Oppression veiled as family honor]. *Noga, 9,* 8–13.

El Saudi, N. (1988). ‏מאחורי הרעלה: נשים בעולם הערבי‎ [Behind the veil: Women in the Arab world]. Givatayim, Israel: Massada Press.

Fenster, T. (1999). Space for gender: Cultural roles of the forbidden and the permitted. *Environment and Planning Society and Space, 17,* 227–246.

Freire, P. (1998). *Pedagogy of freedom.* Maryland: Rowman and Littlefield.

Gamble, J. (2006). *A developmental evaluation primer.* J.W. Mc Connell Family Foundation. Retrieved from http://thepod.cfccanada.ca/sites/thepod.cfccanada.ca/files/A%20Developmental%20Evaluation%20Primer%20-%20McConnell%20Foundation.pdf

Goodlad, J. I. (1987). *Ecology of school renewal.* Chicago, IL: University of Chicago Press.

Gradus, Y., & Abu-Bader, S. (Eds.). (2011). ‏ספר הנתונים הסטטיסטיים על הבדווים בנגב, מס׳ 3‎ [Facts and statistics about the Bedouin in the Negev, no. 3]. Beersheba, Israel: The Robert Arnow Center for Bedouin Studies and Development and the Negev Center for Regional Development.

Gruber, M. I. (1989). Breast-feeding practices in Biblical Israel and in Old Babylonian Mesopotamia. *Janes, 19,* 83–61.

Marks, A. (1974). ‏החברה הבדווית בנגב‎. [The Bedouin society in the Negev]. Tel Aviv, Israel: Reshafim.

Meir, A., & Barnea, D. (1986). ‏התפתחות מערכת החינוך הבדואית בנגב‎ [The development of the Bedouin educational system in the Negev]. Beersheba, Israel: Ben Gurion University.

Patton, M. Q. (2011). *Developmental evaluation: Applying complexity concepts to enhance innovation and use.* New York, NY: The Guilford Press.

Reinharz, S. (1992). *Feminist methods in social research.* New York, NY: Oxford University Press.

Schon, D. (1983). *The reflective practitioner.* USA: Basic Books.

Swirsky, S., & Hasson, Y. (2005). *אזרחים שקופים* [Transparent citizens]. Tel Aviv, Israel: Mercaz Adva.

Tal, S. (1995). *האשה הבדואית בנגב בעידן של תמורות* [The Bedouin women in the Negev in an era of change]. Beersheba, Israel: The Joe Alon Center.

Westley, F., Zimmerman, B., & Patton, M. (2007). *Getting to maybe*. Canada: Random House.

JUDITH ZAMIR *is the head of the Evaluation Department at Kaye Academic College for Education and a lecturer in sociology and counseling.*

SALEEM ABU JABER *is the head of the Training Program for Elementary Teachers in the Bedouin Population, director of the Center for Research in the Teaching of Arabic Language and Literature, and a senior lecturer in Arabic language and literature and Islamic culture at Kaye Academic College for Education, Beersheva, Israel.*

Zoabi, Kh., & Awad, Y. (2015). The role of evaluation in affirmative action-type programs. In B. Rosenstein & H. Desivilya Syna (Eds.), *Evaluation and social justice in complex sociopolitical contexts. New Directions for Evaluation, 146,* 83–93.

7

The Role of Evaluation in Affirmative Action–Type Programs

Khawla Zoabi, Yaser Awad

Abstract

This article analyzes two cases of evaluation programs involving the Palestinian minority in Israel from the perspective of social justice and responsibility. The first focuses on the evaluation of a Pre-Academic Preparatory Program (PAPP) of minority students in Sakhnin College. The second focuses on the evaluation of Equal Opportunities for Arab Minority Students at the Technion–Israel Institute of Technology. This article concludes that evaluation could be conceptualized as a promoter of social justice. The article suggests that the contribution of participatory–responsive evaluation is limited and maybe marginal. The article concludes that evaluation for social justice should be only a step in a longer process, which should feed into decision making afterward in order to change and improve policies and programs, as the case of PAPP suggests. Eventually, we conclude that evaluation played a role in promoting social justice in both systems. © 2015 Wiley Periodicals, Inc., and the American Evaluation Association.

One major purpose of evaluation is to promote social changes, empowerment of marginalized groups, and social justice (Chouinard, 2014; Hopson, 2001; Lincoln, 1993; Mertens, 2002; Segerholm, 2001). Abma and Widdershoven (2008) suggest that in order to help effect the kinds of social changes desired, the evaluator establishes certain kinds of relationships with the marginalized population, which are accepting, respectful, and reciprocal in order to help promote the overall social change desired. Thus, responsive evaluators criticize power inequalities and act as advocates of a particular, silenced, and marginalized group against domination, oppression, and injustice. Through the evaluation process and its results, they seek engagement to empower people, as well as to enlarge people's abilities to govern their own lives on individual and collective levels. Yet, the inclusion of a marginalized group in the evaluation process does not guarantee that values like equality and social justice will be prominent (Segerholm, 2001).

Evaluation is a politicized practice that has social and political consequences for the disadvantaged groups and their everyday life and issues of justice. Apparently, evaluation is far from being "value-free"; rather, it is a sociopolitical process that is related to resource allocations and social priorities (Chouinard & Cousins, 2009; Greene, 2000, 2005; SenGupta, Hopson, & Thompson-Robinson, 2004).

Following Rawls, who suggests in *A Theory of Justice* (1971) that everyone has an equal right to basic liberties and equality and that social and economic inequalities, where necessary, should be distributed to benefit the least advantaged people (Connolly & Steil, 2009, p. 3), Sen (1999) and Nussbaum (2000) emphasize that justice includes the capabilities to maintain political and material control over one's environment. Thus, social justice for disadvantaged and marginalized groups is about enhancing their equality and control over their social, political, and economic life.

This article analyzes two evaluations of programs concerning the Palestinian minority in Israel. The first case focuses on the evaluation of a preparatory program of minority students in Sakhnin College. The second focuses on the evaluation of equal opportunities for Arab minority students at the Technion–Israel Institute of Technology, one of the most prestigious academic institutions in Israel.

Both programs have been evaluated from the students' perspective. Explicitly, we used a participative–responsive evaluation model to examine the participants' perceptions regarding these programs, where issues of empowerment and justice are at the heart of this examination. Through the empirical work, we asked the students about their perceptions regarding issues related to empowerment, equality, and justice.

This article argues that when formal institutions acknowledge inequality and injustice of a disadvantaged group and involve them through a process of responsive–participatory evaluation, the potential to improve their social conditions and generate justice may be enhanced. Moreover, this formal recognition regarding the unjust conditions empowers the members of a disadvantaged group and may decrease feelings of alienation and increase motivation and capacity to change their status.

The next section illuminates the social and political context of the study and the Palestinian minority in Israel. Then, we present the two cases. In the last section, we conclude with a discussion of the implications for the role of evaluation in promoting social justice.

NEW DIRECTIONS FOR EVALUATION • DOI: 10.1002/ev

The Social and Political Contexts of the Study

The Arab Palestinian minority in Israel is an indigenous minority that was the majority in Palestine until the establishment of Israel in 1948. The Israeli–Arab War that erupted in Palestine in 1948 resulted in the establishment of the state of Israel and the dispossession and displacement of some 780,000 Palestinians (Abu Lughod, 1971, 153–161). Of the previous Palestinian population of the territory incorporated into the state of Israel, only 156,000 Palestinians remained within the new state and became Israeli citizens. Thus, the overwhelming Palestinian majority of pre-1948 Palestine was transformed almost overnight into Israel's Palestinian minority. Today, Israel has approximately 1.6 million Palestinian citizens, constituting 20% of the country's total population of 8 million (Israel's Central Bureau of Statistics, 2014). The Palestinian minority in Israel belongs to three religions: Muslims make up 82%, while Christians and Druze are at 9% each (Israel's Central Bureau of Statistics, 2014).

The main characteristics of the socioeconomic conditions of Palestinians in Israel are reflected in the fact that the rate of poverty among their households is approximately 53.5%, while among Jewish households the poverty rate is about 14.2%. About 85% of Arab towns are ranked at the fourth lowest socioeconomic development level of the Central Bureau of Statistics. Economic gaps between Jews and Arabs are particularly striking in the data and poverty statistics.

The Palestinian minority in Israel is barely represented in the central government and, aside from a few exceptional cases, elected Palestinian representatives and their parties have never been invited to participate in a governmental coalition. As a result, the interests of the Palestinians in general, and their cities in particular, are not represented in the central government or its powerful ministries. Although Palestinian inhabitants have the right to vote, to be elected to the Knesset, and to elect their local councils, and although there are representatives of their political parties serving in the Knesset, real and influential participation is limited.

The Two Case Studies

This section presents the two cases: The Pre-Academic Preparatory Program (PAPP) at Sakhnin College and the Technion case. Each case has its own evaluation objectives, methods, characteristics, and findings.

Case 1: The Pre-Academic Preparatory Program

The aim of the evaluation study in this case was to evaluate a pre-academic preparatory program from the students' perspective. The evaluation examines the association between the preparatory program and the students' sense of empowerment. We assume that the degree of such a sense of empowerment is a true measure of the success of the pre-academic program.

NEW DIRECTIONS FOR EVALUATION • DOI: 10.1002/ev

The PAPP provides an opportunity to students who, for one reason or another, failed to complete high school but are capable of succeeding and integrating into higher education frameworks. The PAPP is a remedial framework capable, in practice, of bridging gaps that emerge in elementary and high school levels to help strengthen academic abilities and provide students with the tools that they need to pursue higher education. It is an educational framework that offers a second chance for those who did not succeed the first time around (Zoabi, 2012). The uniqueness of the PAPP lies in the fact that students attend it for a set period, then integrate into standard studies at higher education institutions. It raises the students' expectations to do well academically at academic institutions and gives them more confidence in their ability to obtain an academic degree.

Besides countering educational disadvantages, the PAPP also has an explicit social purpose of closing social gaps and enabling those from underprivileged social and economic backgrounds to integrate into the general student population and in higher studies, by increasing the number of students eligible to pursue a university degree. Studies show that most of the applicants for the PAPP come from families of low socioeconomic status (Hyosh, 2000).

In Israel today, there are 46 PAPP frameworks in Jewish communities, accommodating 12,252 students, 6.4% of whom are Arabs (Israel's Central Bureau of Statistics, 2014). The data show that until 2007, only two pre-academic preparatory frameworks catered specifically to Arab students. According to Israel's Central Bureau of Statistics (2014), the percentage of Arab Israelis who applied and failed to enter university in the 2010–2011 academic year stood at 33.6%, while the failure rate among Jewish students was 20.1%. The failure to provide equal opportunities for young Arab adults, coupled with a lack of PAPP frameworks for the Israeli Arab population and high threshold requirements for admission into universities and colleges in sought-after fields, means that many Israeli Arab high school graduates are effectively denied the opportunities for further education.

In view of this state of affairs, in 2009, Sakhnin College established a PAPP framework. The principal aim of the Sakhnin PAPP is to improve access to higher education to high school graduates from Israel's Arab sector by providing a second chance for capable students who wish to pursue a university degree but, for various reasons, did not complete their high school education. It quickly proved very popular, with enrollment growing from 79 students in its first year to 220 students in 2012, 87% of whom were women. Following mutual recognition agreements with many academic institutions in northern Israel, 60% of the program graduates continued their studies at higher education institutions each year.

Our primary aim for this case was to evaluate the extent to which pre-academic preparatory frameworks of this kind contribute to students' internal qualities, beyond the quantitative achievements of their final grades or the percentage of PAPP students who go on to university. To this end, we examined the association between the preparatory program and its students' sense of empowerment. This is especially significant for students at PAPP who had experienced many failures in their lives and came to PAPP with a mass of past disappointments. Thus we focused on a view of social justice including the social and quality of life features behind the academic achievement.

Methods for Case 1. The data collection was based on a questionnaire compiled specifically for the evaluation and consisting of various statements derived from the extensive literature related to empowerment. It should be noted that we found no tool for assessing the effect of academic studies on the individual's sense of empowerment. The questionnaire consisted of two parts. Part I includes demographic and socioeconomic questions. Part II consisted of 53 Likert-type statements linking pre-academic studies with the sense of empowerment. Participants were asked to note the extent to which they agreed with each statement on a 6-point scale from 1 (*Strongly disagree*) to 6 (*Agree very much*), and their opinion on the effect of PAPP studies on their sense of empowerment for each statement, on a 6-point scale, from 1 (*No effect at all*) to 6 (*Affected it a great deal*). The six measures were: reciprocity and relationship with others; personal capabilities; personal goals; a sense of empowerment on managing; dealing with problems and challenges; and a general sense of empowerment.

To ensure that the wording of the statements was clear and well suited to the target population, we asked five judges of content who are knowledgeable on the subject of empowerment to validate the questionnaire.

Study participants and procedure. The study sample consisted of 146 students randomly selected from the pre-university course list at Sakhnin College. The sample represents approximately 71% of the population. The questionnaires were handed out in the classrooms of the college, toward the end of the 2012–2013 academic year. Students answered the questionnaires anonymously. The questionnaires were then reviewed by the researchers.

Findings. The findings reveal a high level of agreement in relation to all six measures of a sense of empowerment, and a high impact of the PAPP studies on the sense of empowerment.

In addition, most students reported a high contribution by the education and empowerment course to both their personal and professional sense of empowerment (95.8% and 95.2%, respectively). Likewise, students reported that the education fundamentals course contributed highly to their professional sense of empowerment (90.3%) and to a moderate degree to their personal sense of empowerment as well (64.0%).

The evaluation study allowed us to make intelligent decisions for structural changes in the program. These changes support the development and empowerment dimension of personality, which increases the students' chances to be accepted at academic institutions—a preliminary condition for upgrading personal, social, and economic levels in the future. Such

NEW DIRECTIONS FOR EVALUATION • DOI: 10.1002/ev

upgrading increases social justice for these students who might remain on the margins of society and deteriorate to undesirable behaviors. The findings of the evaluation showed that the empowerment courses in the PAPP impacted the students to a high degree both on a personal and professional level. However, we found that the foundations of education course had a low impact on the students. Therefore, the foundations of education course was replaced by a course in moral education that exposed students to basic concepts and granted them the knowledge in values education at the theoretical and a practical level. The evaluation contributed through its responsiveness to the students' needs and its ability to generate change and thereby to enhance equal opportunities.

Case 2: Equal Opportunities for Arab Minority Students at the Technion

The Technion, the Israel Institute of Technology established 100 years ago, is the oldest university in Israel. It offers degrees in science, engineering, architecture, medicine, industrial management, and education. The Technion is considered one of the best academic institutions in Israel and a leading institution in the world in the field of engineering and technology.

There are various problems that face Arab minority students at the Technion. A few years ago, the Technion administration decided to acknowledge these problems and to study them through a program aiming eventually at promoting academic success of these students. Consequently, the Technion launched a proactive program among Arab students aiming at addressing the drop-out rate and improving the Arab minority adaptation to the academic life at the Technion. In 2011, the Technion established a new position: assistant to the senior executive vice president for Minority Affairs (ASEVP), and nominated Yosef Jabareen, an Arab, to head this program. As ASEVP, Professor Jabareen developed a specific Program of Equal Opportunities for Arab Minority Students at the Technion.

This intervention program among Arab students was based on four main strategies: (a) reducing drop-out rate; (b) promoting academic excellence; (c) encouraging students to continue second and third degrees; (d) promoting employment in the high-tech sector among those who finished their studies. The aim of this case study is to present and analyze the main results of the evaluation of this program. This case study of evaluation suggests that when the institution acknowledged the inequality and injustice faced by the Arab minority and included them in the process of evaluation, it improved their social conditions and feeling of justice and attachment to place.

The study population at the Technion. Today, there are about 2,000 Arab undergraduate students at the Technion. Since 2000, the number of Arab students at the Technion has doubled, as Figure 7.1 shows. Since 2000, the percentage of Arab students at the Technion has gradually increased

Figure 7.1. Undergraduate Arab Students at the Technion by Years

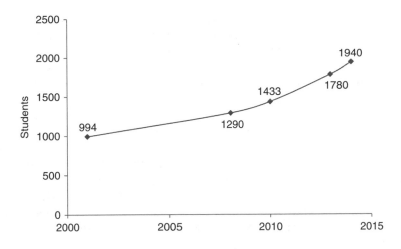

from 11% to about 19% in 2013, to 20% in 2014. There is a steady increase in the number of Arab students who are accepted to the Technion each year. One of the most significant figures regarding the Arab students at the Technion is that about half of them are women, as shown in Figure 7.2, which is a unique characteristic if we compare it to the developing societies around the world.

Methods of Case 2. Data collection was based on a questionnaire which was distributed among 434 Arab students at the Technion. The major components of the questionnaire addressed (a) socioeconomic characteristics; (b) the involvement of the academic program and the lives of individual students; (c) students' attitudes regarding the intervention program, its

Figure 7.2. Arab Students by Gender

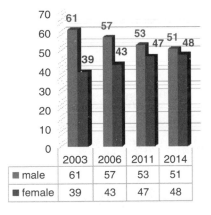

	2003	2006	2011	2014
■ male	61	57	53	51
■ female	39	43	47	48

strengths, and its pitfalls; and (d) recommendations for improvements in the future.

Study participants were given the questionnaires and submitted them to their departments or student dorms by hand. The students filled in the questionnaires personally, and questionnaires were placed in sealed envelopes in order to maintain anonymity and ethical standards. Thus the students were able to report and answer questions freely and without any pressure.

The findings. *1. Major social challenges facing minority students.* The major social challenges that the Arab students face at the Technion, according to the study, were that about 50% of Arab students live below the poverty line (a rate similar to that of the Arab minority in Israel), lack life skills for managing their academic life at the Technion, misunderstand the administrative "rules of the game," and lack knowledge of the "job world."

2. Major academic challenges and achievements. The major social challenges that face the Arab students at the Technion according to the study are:

- High drop-out rate. Yet, as a result of the intervention program, the drop-out rate among Arab students has been decreasing as shown in Figure 7.3.
- Generally, Arab students are not prepared and ready for the academic expectations of the Technion. About 30% of Arab students agreed that they are not studying their "desirable profession" at the Technion. About 60%

Figure 7.3. Dropout Rate Among Arab Students by Year

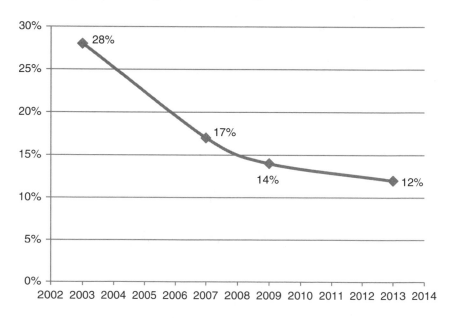

Figure 7.4. Distribution of Arab Students by Departments (Percentage)

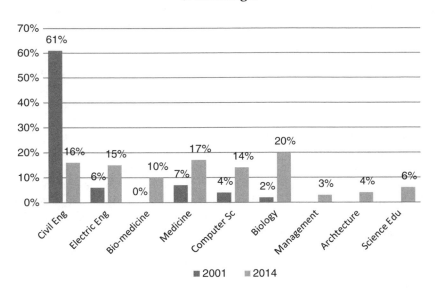

of them reported they did not receive any guidance during their school studies.

- Arab students lack suitable learning skills.
- Arab students face language difficulties.
- The distribution of Arab students by department has been restructured positively and dramatically. Previously, Arab students' main concentration was on civil engineering, and today the Arab students enroll in various and diverse disciplines, as shown in Figure 7.4.

3. Sense of community. Major variables that were examined in the evaluation study included the perception of satisfaction, sense of belonging, and attachment of the Arab students to the Technion.

The majority of the Arab students (84%) agreed that the intervention program of the Technion contributed positively to them specifically and to the Arab students in general. Moreover, the results show that about 70% reported high satisfaction with the learning aspect at the Technion. Yet only 30% expressed satisfaction with feeling "at home" at the Technion, which indicates their feeling of social alienation. It is worth noting that about 81% suggested that they did not participate in any informal activities at the Technion, which indicates a sense of exclusion and alienation.

In sum, the evaluation showed that the intervention program of the Technion among Arab minority students contributed to their academic life, mainly decreasing their drop-out rate and enhancing their academic life at the institution. Yet, it contributed little to their sense of community and feelings of belonging to the Technion as a home.

Discussion: Evaluation as a promoter of social justice. The two cases illustrate the power of the evaluation component of a program in promoting social justice. We used a participative–responsive evaluation model to examine the perceptions of students regarding issues related to empowerment, equality, and justice.

Eventually, we conceptualized evaluation also as a promoter of social justice and empowerment. The evaluation brought to light the significance of a major condition for achieving social justice—the formal institutional recognition of the sources of the problems that face these groups, such as policies of discrimination and racism.

Yet evaluation as a mode of promoting social justice is limited. As one major purpose of evaluation is to promote social changes, empowerment of marginalized groups, and justice, we have to be careful with the limits of the power of evaluation. Evaluation can point out the degree to which a program promotes social justice and where its weaknesses lie. However, it does not always have the power to make changes in that program. This article suggests that the contribution of evaluation as a tool is limited and its contribution maybe marginal, as the Technion case in this study concludes.

Moreover, we believe that evaluation for social justice should be only a step on a longer process; it should feed into the decision-making process in order to change and improve policies and programs.

Evaluation is capable of empowering marginalized people in some ways. In the PAPP study, the findings of the evaluation point to a strong association between a sense of empowerment and the courses offered in the program. The program managers made program changes according to the recommendations of the evaluation. As a result of the changes we found that the percentage of PAPP graduates who integrated into academic studies increased from 35% to 55%. This is a clear example of evaluation promoting social justice and should serve as a model for other evaluation projects.

References

Abma, T., & Widdershoven, G. A. M. (2008). Evaluation and/as social relation. *Evaluation, 14*(2), 209–225.

Abu Lughod, J. (1971). The demographic transformation of Palestine. In I. Abu Lughod (Ed.), *The transformation of Palestine*. Evanston, IL: Northwestern University Press.

Chouinard, J. A. (2014). Understanding relationships in culturally complex evaluation contexts. *Evaluation, 20*(3), 332–347.

Chouinard, J. A., & Cousins, J. B. (2009). A review and synthesis of current research on cross-cultural evaluation. *American Journal of Evaluation, 30*, 457–494.

Connolly, J., & Steil, J. (2009). Introduction: Finding justice in the city. In P. Marcuse, J. Connolly, J. Novey, I. Olivo, C. Potter, & J. Steil (Eds.), *Searching for the just city: Debates in urban theory and practice*. New York, NY: Routledge.

Greene, J. C. (2000). Challenges in practicing deliberative democratic evaluation. In K. E. Ryan & L. DeStefano (Eds.), *Evaluation as a democratic process: Promoting inclusion, dialogue, and deliberation. New Directions for Evaluation, 85*, 27–38.

Greene, J. C. (2005). Evaluators as stewards of the public good. In S. Hood, R. Hopson, & H. Frierson (Eds.), *The role of culture and cultural context: A mandate for inclusion, the discovery of truth, and understanding in evaluative theory and practice* (pp. 7–20). Greenwich, CT: Information Age Publishing.

Hopson, R. K. (2001). Global and local conversations on culture, diversity, and social justice in evaluation: Issues to consider in a 9/11 era. *American Journal of Evaluation*, 22, 375–380.

Hyosh, T. (2000). *Achievements of pre-academic graduates at a teachers college* (Master's thesis). Tel Aviv University, Tel Aviv, Israel.

Israel's Central Bureau of Statistics. (2014). Retrieved from http://www.cbs.gov.il/

Lincoln, Y. S. (1993). I and thou: Method, voice, and roles in research with the silenced. In D. McLaughlin & W. Tierney (Eds.), *Naming silenced lives* (pp. 29–47). New York, NY: Routledge.

Mertens, D. (2002). The evaluator's role in the transformative context. In K. E. Ryan & T. S. Schwandt (Eds.), *Exploring evaluator role and identity* (pp. 103–118). Greenwich, CT: IAP.

Nussbaum, M. (2000). *Women and human development: The capabilities approach*. Cambridge, England.: Cambridge University Press.

Rawls, J. (1971). *A theory of justice*. Cambridge, MA: Belknap Press of Harvard University Press.

Segerholm, C. (2001). Evaluation as responsibility, conscience, and conviction. In K. E. Ryan & T. S. Schwandt (Eds.), *Exploring evaluator role and identity* (pp. 87–102). Greenwich, CT: IAP.

Sen, A. (1999). *Development as freedom*. New York, NY: Alfred A. Knopf.

SenGupta, S., Hopson, R., & Thompson-Robinson, M. (2004). Cultural competence in evaluation: An overview. In M., Thompson-Robinson., R. Hopson, & S. SenGupta (Eds.), *In search of cultural competence in evaluation toward principles and practices*. New Directions for Evaluation, 102, 5–19.

Zoabi, Kh. (2012). Self-esteem and motivation for learning among minority students: A comparison between students of pre-academic and regular programs. *Creative Education*, 3(8).

KHAWLA ZOABI is a visiting scholar and Kreitman Fellow at the Department of Social Work, Ben Gurion University of the Negev and a senior lecturer at the Sakhnin Academic College for Teacher Education, Sakhnin, Israel.

YASER AWAD is a senior lecturer and director of the Center for Professional Development and the Academic Preparatory Program at the Sakhnin Academic College for Teacher Education, Sakhnin, Israel.

Lustig, R., Ben Baruch-Koskas, S., Makhani-Belkin, T., & Hirsch, T. (2015). Evaluation in the Branco Weiss Institute: From social vision to educational practice. In B. Rosenstein & H. Desivilya Syna (Eds.), *Evaluation and social justice in complex sociopolitical contexts. New Directions for Evaluation, 146,* 95–105.

8

Evaluation in the Branco Weiss Institute: From Social Vision to Educational Practice

Ruthie Lustig, Shira Ben Baruch-Koskas, Tova Makhani-Belkin, Tami Hirsch

Abstract

This article presents the unique development of the evaluation unit at the Branco Weiss Institute (BWI) in Jerusalem, an educational nongovernmental organization designed to enhance individual and social growth and to reduce educational gaps in Israeli society. The Institute, which operates a network of schools for at-risk students along with comprehensive high schools, develops and implements educational and social programs in Israel's social and geographic periphery. The article describes the evaluation unit at the Institute as a democratic and culturally responsive mechanism that promotes social justice through the participation of all stakeholders in an ongoing dialogue that generates new knowledge for the organization and its programs. The article includes an illustration of the implementation of the model in a school program for pupils of Ethiopian origin. © 2015 Wiley Periodicals, Inc., and the American Evaluation Association.

The Third Sector in Israel

The third sector (nongovernmental organizations—NGOs) aims to advocate issues of public interest and concern in order to influence government policies. The third sector is community based, and more inclusive and client-focused compared to public welfare organizations or the private sector. This gives the sector a comparative advantage in approaching complex social issues and in reaching marginalized or vulnerable groups (Arvidson, 2009).

In Israel, the third sector performs two primary roles: first, it operates as part of the welfare state system and is funded primarily by the state. Second, it maintains voluntary civil society organizations that provide a framework for individuals to join together in order to address community needs, pursue their collective interests, participate in building society, and foster social change. This aspect of collective life is a major building block of Israel's democratic life.

There are currently more than 34,000 registered third sector organizations in Israel. Most of these are nonprofit associations. The others are funding organizations and advocacy groups. A characteristic feature of the third sector in Israel is the partnership of funding organizations and government.

Israel's third sector emphasizes classic welfare services, with 84% of the sector's economic activity in health, education, and welfare. Public funding is the third sector's main revenue source (55%) (Katz, 2004). In the Hopkins Project's comparisons among 22 countries, Israel ranked fourth, following Holland, Ireland, and Belgium, in the relative size of its third sector within the larger economy.

Evaluation in the Third Sector

Evaluation is becoming increasingly important for governments and donors of the third sector as well as for the organizations themselves (Arvidson, 2009). Although funding agencies are placing increasing demands on organizations to provide evaluations of activities and achievements, they rarely provide resources for organizations to do so (Ellis & Gregory 2009). It is not clear that evaluations are actually used as a basis for decision-making and designing policy. As opposed to focusing on achievements and "results," evaluators in the third sector can promote the idea of outcomes that are not numerical, but rather speak to deeper levels of social change in the individual, school, and community (Reed, Jones, & Irvine, 2005). In addition, an evaluation framework can serve as an instrument for organizational learning. By defining a framework for evaluation, organizations can identify concepts that are essential to their work and suggest theoretical approaches as to how they are related (Sowa, Selden, & Sandfort, 2004).

In general, evaluation faces several challenges. On a managerial level, evaluation requires organizational skills and capacity: fears and expectations of staff have to be managed, and a culture of organizational learning has to be established. The organization should learn how to transform information gained through evaluation processes into organizational learning (Ellis & Gregory, 2009). On a methodological level, it is necessary to understand the possibilities and limitations of different evaluation methods, as well as the difficulties involved with interpreting data. In addition, sometimes the information required by funding agencies does not match the information needs of the third sector organizations. Moreover, there is a tendency to focus on goals and consequently ignore significant unintended outcomes of a program. Another challenge is that when demanding information on outcomes, impacts, and efficiency, funding agencies pay little attention to organizational size and the scope and scale of the work.

The Branco Weiss Institute in the Context of Israeli Society

These challenges become especially prominent in the context of Israel's complex society. Since the establishment of the state, there have been significant demographic changes in Israeli society due to waves of Jewish immigration from different countries. Throughout the years, the socio-cultural–political discourse in Israel has changed from ideology of a society as "melting pot," to a unified Israeli collective identity leaning towards individualism and a multicultural identity. Accordingly, each of the major immigration waves experienced a different welcome, affecting its process of absorption, assimilation, and integration into Israeli society (Sheferman, 2008).

> In 1990, BWI was founded by Dr. Branco Weiss and Dr. Dan Sharon. Its establishment was designed to promote the Israeli education system. A decade ago, the Institute began working directly with youth, both through establishing and operating a network of comprehensive schools and schools for at-risk students and through the implementation of a variety of holistic educational programs within existing schools. The Institute focused its operation in the geographic and social periphery of Israel, with the aim of promoting social justice by closing social and educational gaps. (Branco Weiss Institute, n.d.)

The Institute's use of the concepts *promoting critical and reflexive thinking*, as well as *teaching for understanding*, underlie the assumption that thinking strategies and tools help learners (students and teachers alike) to reach a broader understanding of the world and develop the ability for critical and more flexible attitudes and perceptions. Another assumption is that for students from the periphery, these skills constitute a significant force for progress, integration into society, and the development of leadership capacities. Then they will contribute to social development and promotion of social justice in Israel. To materialize these goals, the Institute established an evaluation unit.

The Evaluation Unit

The internal evaluation unit has been part of the Branco Weiss Institute's (BWI's) organizational structure since 2006. Throughout the years, the evaluation unit's working concept has been formulated and shaped in

NEW DIRECTIONS FOR EVALUATION • DOI: 10.1002/ev

accordance with the organization's evaluative needs as well as its aspiration for organizational learning and improvement. The unit focuses on the usage of evaluation not only as a means of satisfying the stakeholders' need for valuable data, but also as a vehicle for change in the perceptions of the program's second order change circle. This is sometimes not considered as an explicit target of the program. Considering the multiple needs and audiences of an internal evaluation unit, the unit's key principle is an ongoing significant professional dialogue, building trust and partnership amongst the evaluation staff (methodology experts), educational staff (the subject matter experts), commissioners, and stakeholders. The unit's objective is to deliberately enlarge the circle of stakeholders to include society as a whole by using the evaluation research approach as a model to create awareness and social change on the part of the key players in the field.

The evaluation unit is guided in part by a number of principles drawn from conceptual theoretical approaches that reflect the evaluators' commitment to the society in which they operate:

- *Participatory evaluation*, which is based on a cooperative relationship between the evaluator and stakeholders (e.g., Cousins & Whitmore, 1998; Weaver & Cousins, 2004).
- *Responsive evaluation*, which operates within the structural paradigm that conceives of the evaluator's role as an active one, promoting the ongoing dialogue process that includes a variety of perceived realities among stakeholders (Alkin & Christie, 2004). Stake argued that the evaluation "response" is based on three conceptual components (Friedman, 2005, p. 147):
  ○ *Flexibility*—stress on flexibility while performing the evaluation
  ○ *Freedom of action*—granting freedom to the researcher and research program to raise questions and modify the evaluation course
  ○ *Exposure*—full exposure and communication
- *Maintaining an ongoing dialogue between evaluator and stakeholders*, promoting evaluation use (Nevo, 2001). Relevant and useful information can be generated from the existence of constant organizational discourse between the evaluator and the stakeholders (Avgar, Berkowitz, & Shalv-Visgar, 2012). This position is based on the assumption that the evaluation is not a process carried out by the evaluator alone, but a joint endeavor of stakeholders and the evaluator.

This can be created while the different stakeholders are involved in the discourse that accompanies various levels of the research process. This discourse is the basis for creating a constructive partnership between the evaluator and the stakeholders throughout the evaluation process (Alpert, 2010; Nevo, 2001; Patton, 1997). The evaluation unit's unique position as an internal unit allows it to initiate and maintain constant dialog with many of the stakeholders involved in the institute's programs: funding agencies, headquarters, and field staff. Throughout the evaluation process, there is constant dialogue and mutual learning involving the evaluation team and stakeholders. This dialogue takes place with all staff involved in the program, from headquarters to field level (Lustig & Ben Arie, 2013).

For example, every year, each program's findings are presented to the program's managers. In a joint reflection process, the findings are interpreted and form the basis for examining the macro achievements, challenges, and trends regarding the program's goals. The findings are in turn presented to funding agencies and to field staff at different occasions, allowing each setting to conduct important dialogues while gaining insights that can enhance decision making regarding the programs.

The partnership in the evaluation process produces a high level of commitment among the different stakeholders, broadens their perspective on the program and promotes the understanding of each party's contribution and responsibility to the program's achievements, both at the micro and the macro levels. In fact, the evaluation process becomes a significant tool for all stakeholders in maximizing the effectiveness of the programs and promoting its social-educational goals.

The evaluation process produces findings that range over various operating contexts and different periods. The attempt to generate broad ramifications from the findings, while maintaining their relevance, is a continuous process that requires ongoing dialogue between the various stakeholders involved (Ben Baruch-Kuskas, Lustig, & Biran-Zinger, 2013). Such ongoing dialogue plays a crucial role in building deep understanding.

A significant concept in this context is the *blind area* defined by Luft and Ingham (1955) in the Johari Window model as "Knowledge known to others but to not me" (Figure 8.1). Figure 8.1 illustrates the concept of different people being aware of different kinds of knowledge. It is cited here because these differences unconsciously cause different perceptions and understandings of the program and the program's context. Exposing these disparities generates knowledge leading to professional and personal improvement.

The unit's special position within the Institute allows it to have insightful perspectives about the programs operated by the Institute, as well as the various communication channels within the organization. This position enables continuous learning dialogue between the evaluation team, program managers, and field staff. While some of the information about the evaluated programs is relevant only to some of the stakeholders, there are elements to which awareness has a significant effect on the rest of the circles involved. As long as these elements are within the blind area of one of the circles, they are error-prone and their relevance is compromised. The evaluation process is an important facilitator in making covert knowledge into visible knowledge that is part of the shared *open area*. As an internal evaluation unit, the evaluation process is largely aimed toward making the findings accessible

Figure 8.1. Known and Unknown Knowledge Areas in the Johari Window

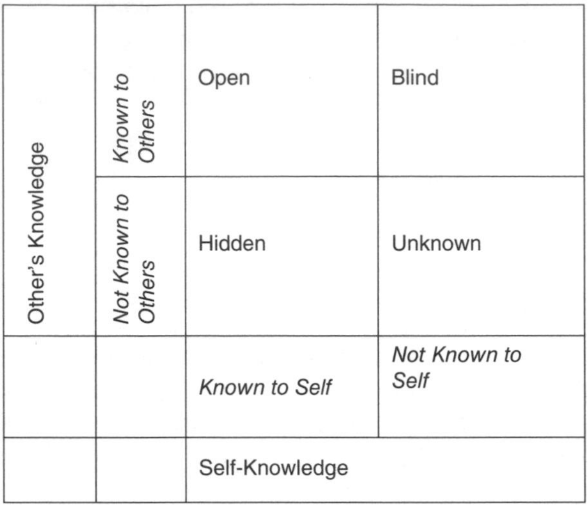

	Known to Others	Open	Blind
	Not Known to Others	Hidden	Unknown
Other's Knowledge		Known to Self	*Not Known to Self*
		Self-Knowledge	

to the different stakeholders, thereby reducing the blind area among them for continued improvement of the programs and realizing its potential.

Contributing to Second Order Change[1]

Most of BWI's programs are funded through partnership with different NGOs that share common values and goals with BWI. Those partners constitute central stakeholders in the progress and the challenges of the programs and in leveraging program achievements for larger scale impact. In addition, the programs work within the Israeli school system—with the collaboration of principals, teachers, and students, making the school system, and on a larger scale, the Ministry of Education, additional important stakeholders. Furthermore, the evaluation unit aims at enlarging the circle of stakeholders to include different key players in the field and society as a whole by using the evaluation research as a basis for creating awareness for social change.

As part of making the findings accessible and useful, many resources are invested in processing them in a user-friendly and relevant way to the different stakeholders. Efforts are made by all parties to adapt the evaluation tools and extend the use of the evaluation findings. For example, every year an effort is made to process the data from the educational programs before the beginning of the following school year, enabling the field staff who are working within schools to receive the findings of their specific school as well as the findings of the total program. The specific information, together with the larger perspective, is then used for drawing conclusions and setting goals for the ensuing annual work plans. The processing and presentation of the findings are tailored to each program based on its needs and goals and are part of annual workshops for the field staff. Throughout, the interpretation process is conducted in collaboration with program managers and staff in joint discussions about the relevant meaning and uses of the findings.

An Example of the Model in Practice

The following example illustrates the evaluation process of one of the BWI programs, which follows up the Institute's program designed for students of Ethiopian origin who study in vocational high schools.

The Jewish Ethiopian immigration to Israel took place in two major waves: 17,000 in the 1980s and 45,000 in the 1990s. Ethiopian immigrants encountered difficulties upon arriving in Israel. A large proportion of the immigrants were uneducated; most of them were farmers, who had a minimum familiarity with educational facilities and modern employment. Ethiopian family structure differs from that of mainstream Israeli families: The number of children is higher, there are many single-parent families with three or more children, and there are many fathers aged over 65 with children under the age of 18. Finally, the absorption of the Ethiopian immigrants took place while Israeli society was facing social, economic, and political challenges: the arrival of a very large wave of immigration from the former Soviet Union, high unemployment rates, a widening social gap, and increased poverty. Over time, feelings of discrimination began to intensify among Ethiopian immigrants. After 20 years, many immigrants of Ethiopian origins have not yet integrated in the Israeli society (Sheferman, 2008).

The schools in this particular program focus on integrating students who dropped out of regular high schools into a learning setting that combines general and vocational studies. The program, funded by the Ethiopian National Project in Israel, operates within the school systems on both individual and systemic levels for helping the Ethiopian youth to graduate and achieve their full scholarly potential while strengthening their personal identity.

In this program, the majority of the work is on a personal–emotional level and focuses on personal–emotional goals, such as self-esteem, motivation, and learning habits. Crucial weight is given to individual work in the schools, both with the students and the teaching staff. One of the special evaluation tools created for the program is a questionnaire for the homeroom teacher of each participant. The questionnaire was designed to gain understanding of the homeroom teacher's perspective concerning the participants during each year and over the years, in comparison to the top functioning level within the class and school. The homeroom teachers complete the questionnaire at the beginning and at the end of each school year. They

NEW DIRECTIONS FOR EVALUATION • DOI: 10.1002/ev

Figure 8.2. Example of an Individual Diagram of a Participant in the Program, in Comparison With the Mean End-of-the-Year Scores of the Participants and Comparison Group

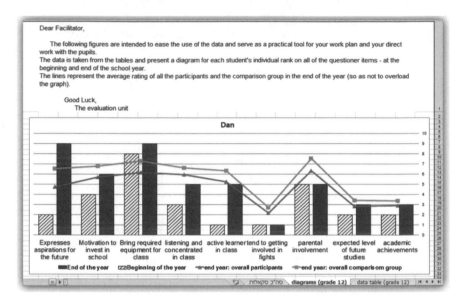

rank each participant on several measures relating to the goals of the program. This information allows monitoring and mapping the participants' needs and progress, and is an important source for identifying areas that require special investment on both individual and group levels. In addition, this instrument facilitates a productive dialogue between the program staff and the homeroom teachers. In addition, as a measure for comparison, the tutors fill out this questionnaire on four other non-Ethiopian-origin students with the highest achievements in the class.

To make the questionnaire a practical and relevant tool, the data are processed on a group level and on an individual basis, giving the program's facilitators an opportunity to review the teacher's perspective on each participant at the beginning and end of the year, compared with all participants in the program and all the pupils in the comparison group (Figure 8.2).

In addition, to enable each facilitator to acquire a broad picture of the program in the school and maximize the potential of his or her dialogue with the school staff, a presentation is prepared for each facilitator, with his or her school's data (Figure 8.3).

Getting the homeroom teachers' perspective on significant characteristics of the participants enables program facilitators to further reduce the blind area by opening a window to an arena in which they are not present. This information enables the creation of a partnership and focused dialogue

Figure 8.3. Example of Findings of the Mean Scores in the Beginning and End of the School Year Among Program Participants and the Comparison Group Regarding Learning Habits

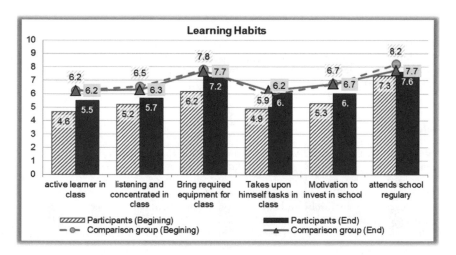

with the teachers regarding their understanding of the participants and the ways to help and promote their progress.

Choosing to process and present the data on an individual basis, in addition to the analysis on the school and overall level, is an investment. It is done to make the data useful—enabling production of shared knowledge that can be used as a practical and relevant work tool throughout the year. The findings become another tool for the facilitators to identify strengths and weaknesses in the school where they work and their individual work with each participant.

Conclusion

This article presents a model of how an internal evaluation unit can influence processes that lead to social change. The model strives to produce synergy among all the stakeholders, including program developers, funding agencies, program operators, participants, and policy makers through an ongoing discourse and learning process. On the one hand, the unit aims at enhancing the Institute as a learning organization. On the other hand, it conducts evaluations of the social and educational programs funded by external funding agencies. While the external funders opt for outcome evaluation, the unit aims at building knowledge and professional capacity. By using the tension created by this potentially problematic situation, the unit serves as a bridge between those agencies, the Institute and all the stakeholders providing a vehicle and an arena for learning and knowledge development. A spiral process is created that surpasses the borders of evaluation and reaches beyond the program itself, narrowing educational and social gaps and disparities in Israeli society. As a result, the target populations are empowered and social justice is promoted.

Note

1. Second order change is creating a new way of seeing things broadly. It requires new learning and questions the organization existing structure (Fox, 1997; Watzlawick, Weakland, & Fisch, 1974).

References

Alkin, M. C., & Christie, C. A. (2004). An evaluation theory tree. In M. C. Alkin (Ed.), *Evaluation roots tracing theorists' views and influences* (pp. 12–65). Thousand Oaks, CA: Sage.

Alpert, B. (2010). Collaboration in evaluation of educational processes: Models and examples between hierarchy and equality. *Studies in Education*, 2-1.

Arvidson, M. (2009). *Impact and evaluation in the UK third sector: Reviewing literature and exploring ideas* (Working Paper 27).Third Sector Research Centre. Retrieved from http://eprints.soton.ac.uk/183217/1/arvidson_working_paper_27.pdf

Avgar, A., Berkowitz, Y., & Shalv-Visgar, Y. (2012). *Building trust in the Israeli education system: Teachers and principals perceptions*. Van Leer Education Conference. (Hebrew). Retrieved from http://itec.vanleer.org.il/Data/UploadedFiles/UserFiles/Emun%20paper%20for%20press.pdf

Ben Baruch-Kuskas, S., Lustig, R., & Biran-Zinger, D. (2013). Narrowing the "blind area": The case of social programs of incorporating and advancing students of the Ethiopian community. In R. Lustig (Ed.), *Evaluators, evaluees and the public: Towards an era of social responsibility* (pp. 18–25). IAPE—Israel Association for Program Evaluation. (Hebrew). Retrieved from the Branco-Weiss Institute website http://www.brancoweiss.org.il/

Ellis, J., & Gregory, T. (2009). *Accountability and learning: Developing monitoring and evaluation in the third sector*. London, England: Charities Evaluation Services, 118.

Fox, S. (1997). *The psychology of resistance to change*. Bar Ilan pub. (Hebrew)

Friedman, Y. (2005). *Measurement and evaluation of social and educational programs*. Jerusalem, Israel: The Henrietta Szold Institute. (Hebrew)

Guba, E., & Lincoln, Y. (1989). *Fourth generation evaluation*. Newbury Park, CA: Sage.

Katz, H. (2004). *The third sector in Israel: Between welfare state and civil society*. Beersheva, Israel: Ben Gurion University, Israeli Center for Third Sector Research. http://bgu.academia.edu/Departments/Israeli_Center_for_Third_Sector_Research_ICTR_

Luft, J., & Ingham, H. (1955). The Johari window, a graphic model of interpersonal awareness. *Proceedings of the western training laboratory in group development*, UCLA.

Lustig, R., & Ben Arie, Y. (2013). Evaluation in the Branco Weiss Institute as a social–organizational discourse (partnership, trust, thinking). In T. Lustig (Ed.), *Evaluators, evaluees, and the public—Towards an era of social responsibility* (pp. 2–8). IAPE—Israel Association for Program Evaluation. (Hebrew)

Nevo, D. (2001). *School based evaluation: A dialogue for school improvement*. Even Yehuda: Reches. (Hebrew)

Patton, M. (1997). *Utilization-focused evaluation*. Thousand Oaks, CA: Sage.

Reed, J., Jones, D., & Irvine, J. (2005). Appreciating impact: Evaluating small voluntary organizations in the United Kingdom. *Voluntas: International Journal of Voluntary and Nonprofit Organizations*, 16(2), 123–141.

Sheferman, K. T. (2008). A portrait of the Israeli public. *The Parliament*, No. 58. The Israel Democracy Institute.

Sowa, J., Selden, S., & Sandfort, J. R. (2004). No longer unmeasurable? A multidimensional integrated model of nonprofit organizational effectiveness. *Nonprofit and Voluntary Sector Quarterly*, 33(4), 711.

Watzlawick, P., Weakland, J., & Fisch, R. (1974) *Change: Principals of problem formation and problem resolution*. Paulo Alto.

Weaver, L., & Cousins, B. (2004). Unpacking the participatory process. *Journal of Multi-Disciplinary Evaluation*, 1, 19–40.

RUTHIE LUSTIG is the head of the evaluation unit at the Branco Weiss Institute and a member of the executive committee of IAPE, the Israeli Association for Program Evaluation.

SHIRA BEN BARUCH-KOSKAS is a researcher in the evaluation unit at the Branco Weiss Institute and a family therapist.

TOVA MAKHANI-BELKIN is a researcher in the evaluation unit at the Branco Weiss Institute.

TAMI HIRSCH is a researcher in the evaluation unit at the Branco Weiss Institute.

NEW DIRECTIONS FOR EVALUATION • DOI: 10.1002/ev

Bitar, K. (2015). Evaluation under occupation: The role of evaluators in protecting and promoting social justice and equality in conflict-affected and fragile contexts (the case of the occupied Palestinian territory). In B. Rosenstein & H. Desivilya Syna (Eds.), *Evaluation and social justice in complex sociopolitical contexts. New Directions for Evaluation, 146,* 107–117.

9

Evaluation Under Occupation: The Role of Evaluators in Protecting and Promoting Social Justice and Equality in Conflict-Affected and Fragile Contexts (The Case of the Occupied Palestinian Territory)

Khalil Bitar

Abstract

The article explicates the conditions in which evaluators in the occupied Palestinian territory (oPt) find themselves due to the realities of the occupation and the conflict-affected and fragile context. It explains the challenges evaluators in the oPt have experienced while conducting evaluations during the last 20 years since the establishment of the Palestinian National Authority in 1994. The evolution of the role of evaluators during the past decade in light of these challenges is presented including what evaluators have been doing to protect and promote social justice, and the strategies used to do so. The article concludes with suggestions on the role evaluators can play in protecting and promoting social justice in other countries in the region and other similar contexts based on the Palestinian experience. © 2015 Wiley Periodicals, Inc., and the American Evaluation Association.

New Directions for Evaluation, no. 146, Summer 2015   © 2015 Wiley Periodicals, Inc., and the American Evaluation Association.   Published online in Wiley Online Library (wileyonlinelibrary.com) • DOI: 10.1002/ev.20124

I n addition to the abounding challenges evaluators often face wherever they work, evaluators in the occupied Palestinian territory (oPt) encounter numerous political, logistical, methodological, and ethical challenges. Many of these challenges are directly linked to the political situation caused by the continuous occupation of the oPt since 1967 and the predominantly volatile political circumstances that have dominated the scene since the failure of the peace process between Israel and the Palestinian Liberation Organization (PLO). Several of the obstacles confronting oPt evaluators are similar to those evaluators in other conflict-affected contexts often experience (see Bush & Duggan, 2013, for a further discussion of the different classification of these challenges in conflict-affected and fragile contexts).

Despite the political situation, and the continued existence of many of the obstacles involved when working in such a challenging context, evaluators in the oPt have made a significant breakthrough in their role during the past decade. Not only have evaluators in the oPt been very active in raising the importance of evaluation in general, but they have been successful in enhancing their role in protecting and promoting social justice and equality as well.

The article draws on the conceptualization of social justice, usually labeled "justice as fairness" (Rawls, 1999). According to Rawls, social justice denotes ensuring and guarding equal access to civil freedoms, human rights, and opportunities, and protecting the least privileged members of society.

Context

In the oPt, the process of state-building began with the establishment of the Palestinian National Authority (PNA) in 1994 after the signing of the Oslo Accords and Agreements between Israel and the PLO. The Oslo framework set out a five-year process to reach a final resolution of the long-lasting Israeli–Palestinian conflict. The framework expired in May 1999 without reaching a resolution of the final status issues. Since then, the international community has introduced a series of peace initiatives. All efforts have failed, however, and the occupation regime has tightened following the eruption of the Second Palestinian Uprising (Intifada) in late September 2000. Since then, the daily life of the Palestinian people has been shaped primarily by the realities of the Israeli occupation.

Following its takeover of Gaza in June 2007, Hamas claimed full control of the Gaza Strip and removed PNA officials. After the takeover, two separate Palestinian governments reigned, one in the West Bank and one in the Gaza Strip. Sanctions imposed against the PNA after Hamas's victory in the Palestinian legislative elections in January 2006 and the formation of the Hamas-led unity government were terminated in the West Bank

This research was not supported by any grant.

after the takeover of Gaza in 2007. In Hamas-controlled Gaza, however, sanctions were replaced by a severe blockade and military measures introduced by Israel, as well as a political and financial boycott by members of the Quartet (the United States, the European Union, the United Nations, and Russia). As some commentators have noted, "the Hamas takeover of the Gaza Strip marked the beginning of a new social, economic, and political era for Palestine" (Qarmout & Beland, 2012, p. 32). Despite the recent reconciliation agreement between Fateh and Hamas signed in April 2014, the West Bank and the Gaza Strip remain politically divided.

East Jerusalem also remains under full Israeli control, isolating the city from the rest of the oPt. The PNA does not have any real sovereignty over the city. The Israeli settlements built on the oPt in the West Bank and East Jerusalem continue to play a major role in complicating the political, economic, and social realities of the Palestinian people. Roadblocks and checkpoints installed from the north to the south of the West Bank by the occupation authority remain one of the most difficult challenges facing the people in the West Bank. Settlements are considered illegal under international law, and members of the international community frequently

Figure 9.1. Map of the West Bank Illustrating Areas A, B, and C

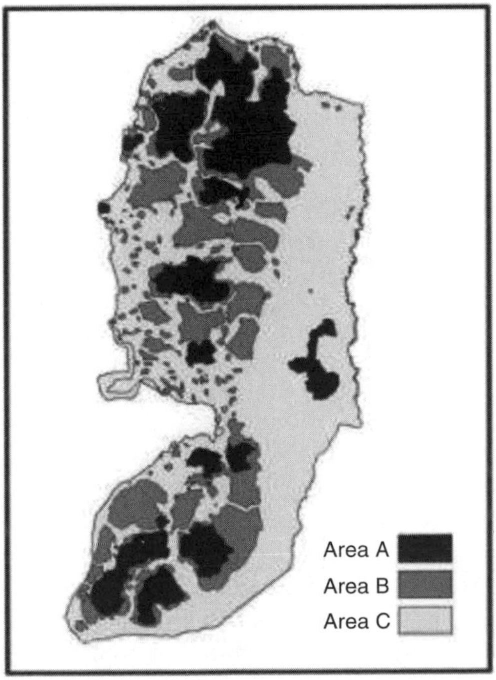

Source: Gordon (2008, p. 178).

condemn their existence and expansion (UNISPAL, 1980). The Israeli separation wall built along and within the West Bank constitutes another significant challenge facing the Palestinian people. Additionally, three district administrative divisions exist in the West Bank: Areas A, B, and C. While Area C[1] represents 61% of the total area of the West Bank and is seen as fundamental to the viability of the future Palestinian state, it is under full Israeli civil and security control (except over Palestinian civilians) and only 1% of it is allocated for Palestinian development (International Labour Organisation, 2012, p. 4). Figure 9.1 illustrates the three district administrative divisions of the West Bank.

The PNA is heavily dependent on foreign aid. Palestinians living in the West Bank and Gaza have been among the world's highest per capita recipients of foreign aid since the signing of the Oslo Accords and the establishment of the PNA in 1994 (Zanotti, 2014, p. 1). Despite this unprecedented volume of foreign aid, the oPt still lags behind most neighboring countries in the MENA region in most social development indicators.

While the oPt did not take an active part in the "Arab Spring" revolutionary movements, a limited number of demonstrations calling for the resignation of the then nondemocratically appointed government in the West Bank were observed in several cities in late 2012. Social justice, equality, and improved economic policies were among the most prominent demands of the protesters. Such protests continued, but on a smaller scale.

Challenges

Against the previously mentioned circumstances, evaluators are greatly needed in the oPt. Their role is not only vital in evaluating the effectiveness of development efforts, but also in protecting and promoting social justice and equality with the ethical responsibility they have as evaluators (Ericson, 1990). Nonetheless, evaluators in the oPt have been faced with several political, logistical, methodological, and ethical challenges that are directly linked to the sociopolitical situation. The next section presents a number of these challenges that are linked to protecting and promoting social justice and equality.

Lack of a Strong Evaluation Culture

Similar to many developing countries, the oPt lacks a strong evaluation culture. When monitoring and evaluation (M&E) units and departments were established in most international, and then national, organizations in Palestine during the early 2000s, they were perceived as a mere donor requirement. Much focus was spent on accountability, rather than on learning. M&E staff and managers were mainly international, coming from the same donor country that financially supported the specific organization, project or program. To many, both the monitoring and evaluation functions, especially evaluation in this case, were seen as no more than a waste of the limited resources to fulfill a donor requirement.

A reverse trend started from the mid-2000s. Policy makers increasingly started to observe the importance of the data and findings provided by their M&E units and departments. In addition, M&E became more prominent internationally after the 2005 Paris Declaration on Aid Effectiveness, which focused on achieving results and the necessity that recipient countries measure these results themselves. Palestinian M&E professionals slowly started to replace their international counterparts in the different projects' and programs' M&E units and departments. M&E units were also established at different governmental institutions, and national development strategies and plans requested that governmental institutions pay more attention to monitoring and evaluating their interventions.

Despite progress, however, evaluation is still not largely accepted, whereas it should be embraced. Many policy makers interpret evaluation as a lack of trust and goodwill when it critiques a certain policy, program, or project. This is especially true for policy makers and implementers, who see the role of evaluation as highlighting successes that could help them in their fundraising efforts.

During the past decade evaluators in the oPt have been playing a significant role to enhance the evaluation culture and promote a more enabling environment for evaluation. The struggle to improve the evaluation culture and principles itself reinforces the place evaluators have while working with other groups and social movements that are calling for enhanced social justice and equality.

Restricted Access and Mobility

As mentioned above, the three main parts of the oPt (the West Bank, the Gaza Strip, and East Jerusalem) are governed by three different authorities. Israel has full sovereignty over East Jerusalem, which it occupied in 1967; the PNA controls parts of the West Bank and Israel controls the rest of it; and finally, Hamas (after the takeover in 2007 and despite the recent reconciliation agreement) still governs the Gaza Strip, but does not control most of its borders. Evaluators in the oPt find it extremely difficult to travel across these three regions. For example, evaluators working in the West Bank cannot travel to Gaza without a prior permit from the Israeli Defense Forces (IDF), the Hamas security forces, and an initial agreement from the PNA in the West Bank. To visit Jerusalem, evaluators in the West Bank need a special permit from the IDF; and evaluators from Gaza find it extremely difficult to obtain the necessary permit from Israel to visit the West Bank or East Jerusalem.

Even within the same area, it is often very difficult to reach the different communities due to political and security related constraints. Generally speaking, Area C of the West Bank is not readily accessed by Palestinian evaluators. Many of the communities adjacent to the Green Line[2] are split into two parts, one in Israel and the other in the West Bank. The separation wall enforces these newly drawn borders.

When planning and conducting evaluations, evaluators in the oPt are confronted with several obstacles due to restricted access and mobility. These can be political, technical, and methodological. For example, the fact that local evaluators are restricted from certain areas and regions causes underrepresentation of a certain population being included during the evaluation. Statistically representative samples are often very difficult to obtain. Key stakeholders to be interviewed cannot be reached by evaluators. Site observations are often limited to restricted areas in which the evaluator works. Even when evaluators ask key informants to come to the areas they have access to, many of them cannot attend due to the restricted mobility and the political and security situations. When key informants manage to attend, however, it often entails a significant increase in the evaluation costs due to additional transportation expenses.

International evaluators who work in the oPt face similar challenges. Nevertheless, they enjoy greater access and mobility than their Palestinian counterparts. Hence, many organizations and institutions might prefer to hire international, rather than local Palestinian, evaluators. While this could be seen as a good solution to the problem of access and mobility and to ensure a more rigorous methodology, in fact the quality of the evaluation could be compromised due to inadequate understanding of the local context by international evaluators. Recently many organizations have started to opt for an evaluation team composed of local and international evaluators. Although this is seen as a good solution, many organizations lack the necessary means and needed financial resources to do so.

The lack of strong evaluation capacity in the oPt is also directly linked to access and mobility. Palestinian evaluators find it extremely difficult to travel, hold meetings, and organize themselves in professional networks. The Palestinian Evaluation Association (PEA), launched in early 2013, constitutes a basis of hope in this regard. Nonetheless, since its inception, the PEA has failed to convene evaluators from the West Bank and Gaza, other than in virtual meetings via the Internet. As a Palestinian organization, and unlike international NGOs and donor agencies, the PEA cannot obtain permits for its members to travel between the West Bank, Gaza, and East Jerusalem.

Occupation as the Scapegoat

The PNA and several local and international NGOs, who often see occupation as the main reason behind any failure, expect evaluators to highlight the impact of the occupation on the degree of success of their policies, programs or projects. This approach allows the implementer to judge any success, even if limited, as greatly significant, and any failure as a natural consequence of the occupation. If evaluators do not agree, and highlight other factors that may explain any shortcomings or failure, despite occupation and its often negative influence, their work might be seen to misunderstand the local context or to underestimate the negative impacts of the Israeli occupation. Hence, evaluation findings are subjected to harsh criticism if they do not include, on the top of the list of findings, the role of the Israeli occupation and its related negative impact. Many evaluations do find that the Israeli occupation indeed proves to have a significant negative influence. In most instances, however, there is a complex interplay of other factors that contribute to the findings. While evaluators like to present these challenges, implementers often focus on the one they like to see topping any list, the negative impact of the occupation.

In many instances, this largely ethical challenge constitutes an important barrier to including findings and recommendations that can highlight what implementers should improve in order to be more effective and to consider social justice and equality aspects of their work. Even when evaluators manage to include such findings and recommendations, and the explanations why implementers could do better despite the political challenges, many implementers often insist on undermining such findings.

Protecting and Promoting Social Justice and Equality

During the first ten years since the establishment of the PNA in 1994, evaluators in the oPt played a rather minimal role in promoting social justice. In fact, evaluators in the oPt played a rather negligible role in development efforts in general between 1994 and 2004. The reasons behind this minimal role include (a) the political and security challenges caused by the occupation and the overall political instability; (b) the small number of evaluation professionals and their limited evaluation capacity; (c) the absence of a network that unites Palestinian evaluators; and (d) the lack of a strong evaluation culture in general. Nonetheless, it has been observed that since 2004, evaluators in the oPt have started to play an increasingly greater role in general and in protecting and promoting social justice and equality in particular. This development in the evaluators' role occurred despite the existence of many of the challenges discussed, most importantly the political and security challenges, due to important developments presented here.

In most evaluations conducted in recent years, evaluators have not been satisfied with merely investigating how successful an intervention is in achieving its set goals and objectives; they have also investigated how well these goals consider social justice and equality issues. Through their evaluation work, evaluators often assess the degree in which different stakeholders and beneficiaries have contributed to the design of the evaluated policy, program, or project. They also assess whether the evaluated policy, program, or project is targeting members of society who are often excluded, most importantly those who live in extreme poverty, people with disabilities, unemployed, refugees, youth, and women members of these groups, as well as women in general.

In their work, evaluators advocate for the use of the equality-focused and gender-responsive evaluation approach, despite resistance from project and program managers and policy makers. They sometimes question evaluators' mandate to do so, claiming that evaluators' role is merely to assess the success or failure of a certain intervention and provide recommendations in this regard.

Indeed, evaluators often find themselves in a relatively weak position to critically assess an intervention based on the degree to which it considers social justice and equality when there is a specific set of evaluation questions precisely asked in the evaluation terms of reference (ToR) and no mention of evaluating the intervention's consideration of social justice and equality issues. Many evaluators started to combat this obstacle by working to enhance the evaluation culture in general, explaining the ethical responsibility evaluators have to critically evaluate any intervention and negotiate evaluation questions as they appear in the ToR if they neglect social justice and equality issues.

Evaluators are not only calling for the inclusion of the neglected segments of society through the evaluation reports they are producing, but they are also publishing opinion articles in some of the most widely read local newspapers and news websites calling for social justice and equality in the overall development efforts that are taking place in the oPt. Advocacy campaigns that aim to open the public's eyes to the significant role of evaluation in protecting and promoting social justice are among the most important techniques used by evaluators to promote both evaluation and the role of evaluation in protecting social justice and equality in the governmental and nongovernmental development interventions.

In addition, many evaluators are becoming less satisfied with merely blaming the occupation for all development challenges in the territory. They are calling for enhanced governmental performance, better donor coordination, and improved interministerial cooperation, according to national plans and priorities. Moreover, while the Palestinian Legislative Council (PLC) has been unable to meet and govern since 2007 due to the Israeli imprisonment of several members, the Fateh–Hamas conflict, and the indefinite postponing of elections by the Fateh leadership in the West Bank and the Hamas leadership in Gaza, efforts have been initiated to work closely with some PLC members to promote evaluation and social justice.

Furthermore, due to the blockade and the political separation between the West Bank and Gaza, Palestinians in the Gaza Strip are often excluded from many of the development interventions that have occurred in the oPt since 2007. Even with interventions that are implemented in both the West Bank and Gaza, managers and policy makers often advise evaluators not to travel to Gaza in order to interview different beneficiaries and stakeholders due to mobility challenges or the dangers evaluators may subject themselves when travelling. Many evaluators in the oPt do not find this approach appropriate, and they are seriously concerned that Palestinians in the Gaza Strip are not benefiting from these development efforts due to political considerations. Hence, many evaluators ask client organizations and institutions to request the occupation authorities to issue entrance permits to Gaza, despite the assumed risks. If these efforts fail, evaluators often try to make contact with key informants in Gaza via the Internet or telephone. Evaluators are currently calling on the PNA, Hamas, and the international donor agencies active in the oPt to put an end to this unequal and unjust treatment of the two parts of Palestine.

Hence evaluators are giving voice to the often-unheard indigent segments of society, and, indeed, reach members of society that many interventions do not. By doing so, evaluators not only play a more significant role through their normal evaluation work, but also as protectors and advocates of social justice, which is often most violated during conflict periods. Ultimately, the efforts evaluators dedicate to protecting and promoting social justice in their communities and countries can arguably lead to a reduction in the level of damage caused by conflict on community members affected.

Conclusions

The past two decades saw the establishment of the PNA and the state building and national development efforts that came with its establishment. This period has also witnessed the failure of the peace process between the PNA and Israel and the tightening of the occupation regime after the Second Palestinian Uprising in late 2000. During the first half of this critical period, the role of evaluators in the overall Palestinian development efforts and in promoting and enhancing social justice was rather minimal. This inconsequential role can be attributed to the abounding political and security challenges caused by the Israeli occupation; the weak evaluation capacity and the limited number of evaluation professionals; the absence of a common entity that unites Palestinian evaluators; and the lack of a strong evaluation culture. Despite the continued presence of many of the political and security challenges, however, the past 10 years saw significant positive developments in the role of evaluators in the oPt in general and in their role in promoting social justice and equality in particular.

In part, the change can be attributed to the enhancement of the evaluation capacity of these evaluators and to the creation of the PEA, an entity that unites evaluators in Palestine, building and sustaining alliances with other evaluators and regional and international evaluation networks, and ultimately enhancing the evaluation culture in the oPt.

This article argues that despite the continued existence of political unrest in the oPt, and in similar conflict-affected situations, evaluators can play a greater role by adopting approaches and strategies that enhance their capacity, better unite their voices, unify their messages, and advance evaluation cultures in their communities and countries. One of the best approaches to achieving such changes can be accomplished through alliances with evaluators and evaluation networks regionally and internationally. Many evaluators no longer feel isolated in their demands and promotion of social justice and equality as they gain much-needed support through the regional and international alliances they build.

Evaluators in other countries, especially in neighboring "Arab Spring" countries and in other conflict-affected and fragile states, may learn from the Palestinian experience in this regard. Palestinian evaluators are disseminating lessons learned through the communities of practice they take part in with their colleagues in the Middle East and North Africa Evaluators Network (EvalMENA), EvalPartners, and the International Organization for Cooperation in Evaluation (IOCE), where protecting and promoting social justice is a central focus.

Notes

1. Area C includes all Israeli settlements (cities, towns, and villages), nearby land, most roadways that connected the settlements (and which are exclusively for Israeli use) as well as strategic areas described as "security zones" by the Israeli occupation forces.

2. The Green Line is a demarcation line set out after the 1949 Armistice Agreements between Israel on the one hand and Egypt, Jordan, Lebanon, and Syria on the other hand after the 1948 War. It is now used to mark the lands Israel occupied during the 1967 Six-Day War, namely, the West Bank, Gaza Strip, and Golan Heights.

References

Bush, K., & Duggan, C. (2013). Evaluation in conflict zones: Methodological and ethical challenges. *Journal of Peacebuilding & Development, 8*(2), 5–25.

Ericson, D. (1990). Social justice, evaluation, and the educational system. *New Directions for Program Evaluation, 45,* 5–21.

Gordon, N. (2008). *Israel's occupation.* Berkeley and Los Angeles, CA: University of California Press.

International Labour Organisation. (2012). *The situation of workers of the occupied Arab territory.* International Labour Conference, 101st Session. Report to the Director-General. ILO Publication No. ILC.101/DG/APP. Geneva, Switzerland: International Labour Organisation.

Qarmout, T., & Beland, D. (2012). The politics of foreign aid to the Gaza Strip. *Journal of Palestinian Studies, 41*(4), 32–47.

Rawls, J. (1999). *A theory of social justice* (2nd rev. ed.). Cambridge, MA: Belknap Press of Harvard Univ. Press.

UNISPAL. (1980). *Security Council Resolution 465* (United Nations Security Council Resolution. United Nations Resolution No. S/RES/465 1 March 1980).

United Nations. (2012). *General Assembly Resolution 67/19* (United Nations General Assembly Resolution. United Nations Resolution No. A/RES/67/19 4 December 2012).

Zanotti, J. (2014). *U.S. foreign aid to the Palestinians* (Congressional Research Service Report. CRS Publication No. 7-5700-RS22967). Washington, DC: Congressional Research Service. Retrieved from http://fas.org/sgp/crs/mideast/RS22967.pdf

Khalil Bitar is a Palestine-based evaluator and an M&E expert and works as an independent consultant with several governmental institutions and local and international nongovernmental organizations in Palestine and the MENA region. He is the founder and director of the Palestinian Evaluation Association.

New Directions for Evaluation • DOI: 10.1002/ev

Steinberg, S., & Zamir, J. (2015). A different light on normalization: Critical theory and responsive evaluation studying social justice in participation practices. In B. Rosenstein & H. Desivilya Syna (Eds.), *Evaluation and social justice in complex sociopolitical contexts. New Directions for Evaluation, 146,* 119–127.

10

Evaluation of a Joint Israeli–Palestinian Project

Shoshana Steinberg, Judith Zamir

Abstract

This article presents three examples of evaluation intervention demonstrating the ongoing significance of a politically responsive approach. The article's main goal is to shed light on the evaluator's role, through the work of a mixed team of Israeli and Palestinian teachers, within a conflict, in an uncomfortable zone context. Israeli and Palestinian teachers participated in a project aimed at producing a history textbook including the narratives of each group, each of whom had its own legitimate objectives. This article intends to highlight the significant contribution of the evaluator to the entire process through the use of three different evaluation tools. © 2015 Wiley Periodicals, Inc., and the American Evaluation Association.

This article presents the role of the evaluator accompanying the work of a group in a conflict zone (Davidson, 2014). According to Davidson, the new conceptions of *justice* have shifted to increased emphasis on the perspectives of participants and other impactees such as women, people of color, and people living in conflict zones. The case discussed here is about Israeli and Palestinian teachers who developed a history textbook including both groups' narratives of the same events presented side by side. There were six teachers in each group. The project was joined and monitored by a developmental evaluator centering on situational sensitivity, responsiveness, and adaptation (Patton, 2011). The goal of the project was to promote understanding between the two groups, which are involved in a long and violent conflict. The goal of the evaluation was to make sense of what emerged under complex conditions, interpreting the dynamics and interactions and unveiling the stories within and behind the process.

The project and its evaluation lasted for seven years, from 2002 to 2009. In this article, we present three different situations in which the evaluator intervened in the group process, thus facilitating the development of the process. Our presentation includes various evaluative approaches that were applied in response to the group's needs at different crossroads of the project. The approaches were used in response to the context intuitively, but have been discussed in the literature as well. Formative evaluation (Scriven, 1967) focuses on the process, whereas developmental evaluation (Patton, 2011) supports innovation development and guides adaptation to dynamic and changing realities. Participatory evaluation (Cousins & Whitmore, 1998) is an approach that is very much concerned with practical problem solving and providing support for ongoing programs. Politically responsive evaluation[1] (Azzam & Levin, 2014) stresses the notion that political factors have as much influence as technical factors on rational decision making; and dialogical evaluation (Dart & Davies, 2003) focuses the direction of work towards explicitly valued directions and away from less-valued directions, challenging the aspiration for a clearly reasoned, well-crafted, and coherent evaluation story (Davidson, 2014). The evaluation continued until the group's mission was completed.

We are aware that many factors contributed to the development of the group and the success of the joint project, in spite of the internal and external barriers. However, in this article we will focus on the contribution of the evaluation process. The article includes examples from the process and an ethnographic description of the interventions that took place during a period of violent conflict between Israelis and Palestinians.

Evaluation Helps Move Through a Crossroads

Some discussions among the teachers were heated, evoked deep emotions, and led to crisis situations. At the beginning, there was disagreement about facts, interpretations, and use of terms. Each side seemed to be sure that its story was "the truth", while the other's was propaganda, deliberate distortion, or at best lack of knowledge. Many discussions led to the feeling of frustration and reached a dead end. These were the crossroads where interventions were needed in order to help the group overcome the crisis situations. The interventions took place in two forums: bi-national and uni-national. Each weekend meeting of the Israeli and Palestinian teachers included a two-hour uni-national forum. The format of uni-national forums evolved from years of experience with encounter groups between

Arab and Jewish Israeli citizens at the School of Peace in Neve Shalom.[2] The facilitators at Neve Shalom came to the conclusion that because each group had different needs, uni-national meetings allowed the participants of each group to raise issues that they preferred not to share with the other group. It helped each group to be better prepared for the bi-national forum (Sonnenschein & Hijazi, 2000). This format was later adopted in other encounter groups. In the Israeli–Palestinian teachers' project, the uni-national meetings were safe places where each group could air their frustrations without taking the risk of insulting the other side. They provided the opportunity for venting, trying to understand the differences in culture, values, and reality of each group. In some instances, there was no need for a direct intervention. Sometimes the evaluator's remark or question helped the group members to better understand the conflict. The following example reflects the evaluator's intervention at the Israeli teachers' uni-national meeting, when a major crisis seemed to threaten the continuation of the project.

It is important to note that the hardest and most challenging discussions took place about recent history, beginning with the 1967 War. The Israeli teachers were upset and disappointed when they read the Palestinian narrative. The Palestinians presented it as the "war of aggression" that was initiated by Israel in order to occupy Palestinian land. The Israelis felt that the Palestinian narrative denied the legitimacy of Israel and its right to exist, and said that those who wrote it "are not for peace, they are for war." The Palestinians, who felt attacked, responded by saying that they have the right to write their narrative the way their people see the reality. The Palestinians were insulted by the Israelis' tone of voice. They expressed anger about what they saw as a power struggle, and an attempt to limit their freedom of self-expression.

The incident is an example of a misunderstanding that can be explained as stemming from the mistrust between the two groups, and their different interpretations of the other's behavior and intentions. The main reason for the Israelis' frustration was the fact that the text was written after two years of cooperation between the two groups. In the uni-national forum, the Israeli teachers said that they expected the Palestinians to use terminology and concepts that may lead to tolerance, peace, and coexistence at such an advanced stage of the group's development. The evaluator clarified the fact that there were two teachers who joined the group recently in the Palestinian team that wrote that chapter. This remark opened a discussion about the high rate of turnover among the Palestinian teachers and its impact on the group process. In the Palestinian team, only two of the original six teachers remained in the project from the beginning until the end, while none of the original Israeli team members left. The Israeli teachers realized that this fact had to be taken into account in their expectations concerning the development of the group. The discussion about the Palestinians' response to their criticism helped them understand the impact of the broader context on group dynamics.

During the bi-national workshop, that took place later, an Israeli teacher apologized for her angry and emotional message. Both sides agreed that at this point in history, in the midst of an ongoing violent conflict, they could not write a harmonious narrative, but since they wanted to write a peace promoting text, a reconciliatory tone should guide them.

Responsiveness and Conceptualization

The following example of the evaluator's responsiveness to participants' needs also relates to expectations about group development. In the uninational forum, the Israeli teachers frequently expressed disappointment with the group process. There were many situations that they interpreted as signs of lack of progress in the development of trust and mutual understanding. They were especially frustrated with regressions that appeared after periods of cooperation, listening to each other, and taking into account the other group's needs.

The evaluator introduced two models of group developmental processes: one linear and one chaotic. The first model presents a linear process of development in stages, as could be inferred from contact theory (Allport, 1954). The second model presents chaotic changes, as one could infer from the point of view of the conflict group model, as practiced by Neve Shalom (Sonnenschein, Halabi, & Friedman, 1998), where the group process is an interaction between the pressure of the conflict reality outside the group and the internal group process. Therefore a linear process cannot be expected to take place based only on the internal group process.

The Israeli teachers appreciated the theoretical input of the evaluator, which they found helpful and thought provoking. They asked for reading material and discussions on relevant topics. The evaluator referred them to an article that introduces a typology for discourse classification (Steinberg & Bar-On, 2002). The typology is a research tool for analyzing the developmental process of discourse in groups in conflict. Development is defined as changes in the quality of discourse, progressing on a scale from the lowest point, "ethnocentric talk," to the highest point, "dialogic moment." Progress is transition from discourse based on stereotypes, not listening to the other, and perceiving the other as an object for persuasion, to dialogue characterized by equality, listening, trying to understand reality from the other's point of view, and a joint effort in construction of meaning. It is based on the assumption that change in the quality of discourse is a sign of a cognitive and affective change in the way one perceives the "other," the "self," and "truth," which enables the parties to engage in dialogue and achieve understanding. The instrument can enable observers and researchers to follow the group process and identify development of intergroup communication.

The teachers found the typology useful in gaining insight into the quality of discourse in the group, and became more aware of their side's contribution to changes that may or may not be occurring.

It is important to note that the Palestinian teachers did not express interest in theoretical learning. They seemed to be more task oriented and concentrated on achieving the goal of writing the textbook. For the Palestinian teachers, the project had a very important role. They saw it as a patriotic mission. The teachers stressed that since there was never a Palestinian independent state, this was the first time that Palestinians had an opportunity to make their voice heard. This was the first time that the Palestinian narrative was told. Until the 1967 War, Palestinian children who lived in the West Bank learned Jordanian history, while those who lived in Gaza learned Egyptian history. The teachers who participated in the project were under heavy pressure from their community not to cooperate with the "Israeli enemy." The evaluator understood the asymmetrical conditions of the two groups. Although neither group received support from their communities for participating in the joint project, the Palestinian teachers' reality was harder. Some were threatened with being boycotted or even being physically harmed.

The Israeli teachers did not have to deal with such threats. However, their colleagues and friends did not believe that the effort invested in the project was worthwhile. They were also told by their supervisors that they were not allowed to teach the texts that they wrote in the first booklet that had already been published (PRIME, 2003). The teachers were threatened with the loss of their jobs if they let their students read a textbook that was not approved by the Ministry of Education. The Israelis were annoyed by their supervisors' lack of appreciation of the educational value of the dual-narrative project. However, they strongly believed that the textbook would be approved in the future, and would contribute to building peace. In addition, the teachers viewed the collaboration with their Palestinian colleagues as a unique learning experience.

The evaluator's situational sensitivity and adaptation to the two groups' different needs resulted in an intervention that may have contributed to better quality of communication between the participants. After reading and discussing the article about the typology for discourse classification, the teachers made a conscious effort to improve the quality of discourse during the meetings.

One example of improvement in the quality of communication is a conversation that took place during the 13th group meeting. An Israeli teacher asked his Palestinian colleague, "What do you want my students to know about your narrative?" From the Palestinian teacher's response, it was obvious that the Palestinian teacher appreciated this question. He stressed what he believed that Israeli students should know about Palestinian history from the Palestinians' point of view. The atmosphere was friendly and professional. At the same meeting, a Palestinian teacher asked his Israeli colleague to explain the roots of anti-Semitism in Europe. These examples were very different from the discussions that took place in former meetings. Since the beginning, in spite of knowing that they were going to present two narratives, the teachers did not understand fully that what they were going to hear was very different from what they imagined about the other. For a long period of time each side believed that it knew the "truth." They tried to provide the "right" information, to correct the other's claims, to persuade the other that they were right, in order to make the other think the way they do. The social psychological term for this phenomenon is *naïve realism* (Ross & Ward, 1996). According to Ross and Ward, people tend to believe that they see reality the way it is. If the others do not agree with them, it is because they do not have enough information, or the information that they have is not right, or they distort the facts on purpose, or their ideology blinds them.

For a long time, the teachers' discourse could be classified as *ethnocentric talk*—two monologues that did not meet (Steinberg & Bar-On, 2002). In the examples provided in this article, we can see that the teachers asked questions in order to understand the others better, and took into account the others' needs and feelings. The improvement in the quality of intergroup discourse may be attributed to many factors, such as three seminars abroad, far away from every day pressures, that provided opportunities for the Israelis and Palestinians to get to know each other on a personal basis, develop friendships, break stereotypes, and recognize the complexity of the other. However, the teachers' use of terms that they adopted from learning the typology can be seen as the evaluator's contribution to their awareness of different ways of communicating with the other.

Participatory Evaluation

After six years of meetings, the teachers planned how each would teach the other's narrative in the classroom. The following conversation took place.

> Palestinian teacher: When I teach my class, I need to understand why you think the way you do. I do not understand why the Holocaust has an impact on us, because the Zionist movement had a plan, without a connection to the Holocaust. We have to think about it more, because I do not understand it.

> Israeli teacher: We still feel like victims. It is relevant to understand the Israeli fears.

> Palestinian teacher: We say that the goal of the Zionist movement was decided in Basle: to establish a strong state economically, culturally, military. It was much earlier.

> Israeli teacher: Yes, but in the present the Holocaust is very strong in Israeli society. Jews in Israel feel like victims. It is an explanation of why we are here.

NEW DIRECTIONS FOR EVALUATION • DOI: 10.1002/ev

At this stage, the evaluator felt that the Israeli teachers had not suc-
ceeded in explaining the link between the Holocaust and the establishment of the State of Israel. On this issue, many Israelis do not agree among
themselves. Some stress the Zionist movement as a national movement that
emerged out of a need to stop Jewish suffering in the Diaspora, and the
Balfour declaration that expressed the support of the British government
for establishing a national home for them in the land of Israel. From their
point of view, the Holocaust was not the reason for the Jewish people to
start building the basis for a national state. Other Israelis see the tragic results of the Holocaust as the reason for the UN resolution in 1947 about
the establishment of the State of Israel, which became the home for those
who survived the atrocities but lost their families and homes. The evaluator
chose to participate in the discussion.

> Evaluator: I will tell you a personal story. My parents' families lived in Poland
> for generations. My parents were not Zionists. They saw themselves as Polish
> citizens, connected to the place and the Polish culture. When the Germans
> invaded Poland, they were a young couple with a son who was three-and-
> one-half years old. They escaped to Russia. When they returned to Poland
> six years later, after the war was over, they discovered that their entire family
> was murdered: parents who were in their fifties, brothers and sisters with
> their families—no one survived. A Polish family lived in their home with
> their furniture and everything. They were not let in to take anything. My
> parents went to Israel, because they did not feel that they could live in Poland
> any more. There were many people like them, who came to Israel after the
> Holocaust not because of Zionist ideology.

> Palestinian teacher: I always saw it as an excuse, the use of the Holocaust to
> explain why Jews came here. We should talk more. I want to understand in
> order to be able to explain to my students.

The evaluator perceived the above example as a sign of significant advancement in the quality of discourse in the group that occurred over time.
Researchers in the field of interpersonal and intergroup communication
stress that the illusion of understanding is a main obstacle to understanding,
especially in groups in conflict (Goldman, 2000; Gurevitch, 1989). People explain other people's behavior and intentions using their own frame
of reference, life experience, and assumptions as to what is right, logical,
moral, and just. They do not take into account the others' culture, values,
needs, and perspectives, which shape the way they perceive reality. Peoples'
judgments about the other are based on stereotypic views. This assumption
of "knowing," based on stereotypic definitions contributes to conducting
two monologues that do not meet. Recognition of the distance between
the self and the other, and the ability "to not understand," is a necessary
step towards dialogue that may lead to understanding (Gurevitch, 1989).

The evaluator felt she had facilitated the communication between the two groups through her personal story. It was obvious that the use of a personal story evoked deeper listening and a better understanding of the other's experience. At this stage of the group development, the sixth year of working together, realizing that they did not understand the other was a significant achievement of the project participants.

Conclusion

Abandoning the illusion of understanding the other and reality, as well as the development of the awareness of complexity and the need to listen and learn, occurred in both national groups, as we can see in the following example:

An Israeli teacher who participated in the project was invited to speak about his experience to university students. After he finished his lecture, he was asked what he gained from being involved in the project. He answered, "I learned that I do not understand the Palestinians," and added, "I learned to listen to them in order to understand."

We can sum up the contribution of evaluation to the developmental process of dialogue in the group as related both to direct interventions such as exposing the participants to theoretical reading materials, presenting relevant evidence, sharing personal stories and through indirect means such as modeling desired behaviors of listening to all the voices, asking questions in order to learn about the other's experiences, feelings, and ways of understanding reality.

The politically responsive evaluation framework, as proposed by Azzam and Levin (2014), is concerned with the balance between technical demands and stakeholder needs. They claim that if this balance is attained, then the evaluation achieves political credibility. The evaluation work that has been presented here is much more complex. It is not only a case of balance between technical demands and stakeholder needs, but a balance exercised on the side of the evaluator's analysis of the needs and inputs made by two groups in deep conflict with different interpretations of "reality." The project reflects a great effort to understand the entire, complex political environment that stakeholders occupy, trying to help to avoid asymmetrical power relationships along the process (Azzam & Levin, 2014). The evaluator's awareness leads to the recognition and identification of needs and thinking patterns, translating them to an ongoing/changing response in terms of developmental, participative, and sensitive tools, activities, and models. Use of these interventions moves the process forward, promoting social justice by allowing the voice of all the participants to be heard.

Notes

1. A new concept introduced by Azzam in Azzam and Levin (2014).

NEW DIRECTIONS FOR EVALUATION • DOI: 10.1002/ev

2. Neve Shalom is the only cooperative Jewish–Arab village in Israel. The School of Peace conducts workshops, interventions, and professional training in working through conflicts using group processes. It includes a staff that consists of Jewish and Palestinian Israeli citizens.

References

Allport, G. W. (1954). *The nature of prejudice.* Reading, MA: Addison-Wesley.

Azzam, T., & Levin, B. (2014). Negotiating truth, beauty, and justice: A politically responsive approach. In J. C. Griffith & B. Montrosse-Moorhead (Eds), *Revisiting truth, beauty and justice: Evaluating with validity in the 21st century. New Directions for Evaluation, 142,* 57–70.

Cousins, J. B., & Whitmore, E. (1998). Framing participatory evaluation. In E. Whitmore (Ed.), *Understanding and practicing participatory evaluation. New Directions in Evaluation, 80,* 3–23.

Dart, J. J., & Davies, R. J. (2003). A dialogical story-based evaluation tool: The most significant change technique. *American Journal of Evaluation, 24,* 137–155.

Davidson, E. J. (2014). How "beauty" can bring truth and justice to life. In J. C. Griffith and B. Montrosse-Moorhead (Eds.), *Revisiting truth, beauty and justice: Evaluating with validity in the 21st century. New Directions for Evaluation, 142,* 31–43.

Goldman, M. (2000). Additional reflections on empathy. *Alpayim, 19,* 63–77. (In Hebrew)

Gurevitch, Z. D. (1989). The power of not understanding: The meeting of conflicting identities. *The Journal of Applied Behavioral Science, 25*(2), 161–173.

Patton, M. Q. (2011) *Developmental evaluation: Applying complexity concepts to enhance innovation and use.* New York, NY: Guilford Press.

PRIME. (2003). *Learning the other's historical narrative: Palestinians and Israelis.* Beit Jalah, PNA: PRIME Publication.

Ross, L., & Ward, A. (1996). Naïve realism in everyday life: Implications for social conflict and misunderstanding. In T. Brown, E. Reed, & E. Turiel (Eds.). *Values and knowledge* (pp. 103–135). Hillsdale, NJ: Erlbaum.

Scriven, M. (1967). The methodology of evaluation. In R. Tyler, R. Gagne, & M. Scriven (Eds.), *Perspectives on curriculum evaluation.* AERA Monograph Series—Curriculum Evaluation. Chicago, IL: Rand McNally & Co.

Sonnenschein, N., Halabi, R., & Friedman, A. (1998). Israeli–Palestinian workshops: Legitimation of national identity and change in power relations. In E. Weiner (Ed.), *The handbook of coexsistence* (pp. 600–614). New York, NY: The Continuum.

Sonnenschein, N., & Hijazi, A. (2000). "Home Group": The uni-national forum in the Jewish-Arab encounter. In R. Halabi (Ed.), *Identities in dialogue* (pp. 131–150). Tel Aviv, Israel: Hakibbutz Hameuhad Publishing. (In Hebrew)

Steinberg, S., & Bar-On, D. (2002). An analysis of the group process in encounters between Jews and Palestinians using a typology for discourse classification. *International Journal of Intercultural Relations, 26*(2), 199–214.

SHOSHANA STEINBERG *is a senior lecturer at the Kaye Academic College of Education, Beersheva, and in the Conflict Management & Resolution Program at Ben Gurion University of the Negev.*

JUDITH ZAMIR *is the head of the Evaluation Department at Kaye Academic College for Education, a lecturer in sociology and counseling, and a member of the executive of IAPE: Israeli Association for Program Evaluation.*

INDEX

NEW DIRECTIONS FOR EVALUATION

ORDER FORM SUBSCRIPTION AND SINGLE ISSUES

DISCOUNTED BACK ISSUES:

Use this form to receive 20% off all back issues of *New Directions for Evaluation*.
All single issues priced at **$23.20** (normally $29.00)

TITLE	ISSUE NO.	ISBN

*Call 1-800-835-6770 or see mailing instructions below. When calling, mention the promotional code JBNND
to receive your discount. For a complete list of issues, please visit www.josseybass.com/go/ev*

SUBSCRIPTIONS: (1 YEAR, 4 ISSUES)

☐ New Order   ☐ Renewal

U.S.	☐ Individual: $89	☐ Institutional: $358
CANADA/MEXICO	☐ Individual: $89	☐ Institutional: $398
ALL OTHERS	☐ Individual: $113	☐ Institutional: $432

*Call 1-800-835-6770 or see mailing and pricing instructions below.
Online subscriptions are available at www.onlinelibrary.wiley.com*

ORDER TOTALS:

Issue / Subscription Amount: $ _____

Shipping Amount: $ _____
(for single issues only – subscription prices include shipping)

Total Amount: $ _____

SHIPPING CHARGES:

First Item	$6.00
Each Add'l Item	$2.00

*(No sales tax for U.S. subscriptions. Canadian residents, add GST for subscription orders. Individual rate subscriptions must
be paid by personal check or credit card. Individual rate subscriptions may not be resold as library copies.)*

BILLING & SHIPPING INFORMATION:

☐ **PAYMENT ENCLOSED:** *(U.S. check or money order only. All payments must be in U.S. dollars.)*

☐ **CREDIT CARD:**   ☐ VISA   ☐ MC   ☐ AMEX

Card number _____ Exp. Date _____

Card Holder Name _____ Card Issue # _____

Signature _____ Day Phone _____

☐ **BILL ME:** *(U.S. institutional orders only. Purchase order required.)*

Purchase order # _____
　　　　　　　　Federal Tax ID 13559302 • GST 89102-8052

Name _____

Address _____

Phone _____ E-mail _____

Copy or detach page and send to: **John Wiley & Sons, One Montgomery Street, Suite 1000,
San Francisco, CA 94104-4594**

Order Form can also be faxed to: **888-481-2665**

PROMO JBNND